Welcome to the Bible

Vicki K. Black
and
Peter W. Wenner

MOREHOUSE PUBLISHING

An imprint of Church Publishing Incorporated
Harrisburg — New York

Morehouse Publishing, 4775 Linglestown Road, Harrisburg, PA 17105

Morehouse Publishing, 445 Fifth Avenue, New York, NY 10016

Morehouse Publishing is an imprint of Church Publishing Incorporated.

Cover design by Corey Kent

Library of Congress Cataloging-in-Publication Data

Black, Vicki K.
    Welcome to the Bible / Vicki K. Black and Peter W. Wenner.
        p. cm.
    Includes bibliographical references.
    ISBN 978-0-8192-2236-7 (pbk.)
    1. Bible—Introductions. I. Wenner, Peter W. II. Title.
    BS475.3.B54 2007
    220.088'283—dc22   2007008612

Printed in the United States of America

07 08 09 10 11 12   10 9 8 7 6 5 4 3 2 1

For Constance Jean Moon and
Herbert A. Wenner, M.D.

Contents

Introduction

The Bible can be an intimidating book. It is big—well over a thousand pages. It is difficult reading. It has a reputation. Those three strikes against it can deter many of us from even getting started reading the book. And, even if we do begin to read, we quickly encounter cultural and literary expressions that are unfamiliar and off-putting. This is true for people of faith as well as for those who simply want to know more about the book that has inspired much of western literature and has influenced three of the world's largest religions.

In this small introduction to the Bible, we invite you to begin reading that intimidating, important—and inspiring—book of faith. We will describe the Bible and its literature, offer a perspective on its theological and religious meanings over time, and make some suggestions about how to read and study it. Our hope is to make the Bible more accessible and intelligible to people who are exploring a deeper relationship with God in Jesus Christ, whether you have been in the church for years or are just beginning in the Christian faith.

Our approach to the Bible is based on our regular and disciplined reading of Scripture over many years. As clergy in the Episcopal Church we have had some training in biblical studies and theological reflection, but such training is not a prerequisite for opening the pages of the Bible and profiting from what is encountered there. Certainly an informed study of current biblical scholarship will enhance and deepen an understanding of the Bible; but it is also important to approach the Bible on its own, to become familiar with the stories of Scripture, and to allow the Bible to become a part of our experience. A personal knowledge of the Bible and its stories can then form a solid basis for further study and scholarship, as we begin to look deeper and ask more searching questions.

People approach the Bible in a variety of ways and with many different purposes in mind. Some read it for the beauty of its literature: its poetry, its sagas, its sweeping theologies. Others like to mine the Bible for teaching and instruction. Some seek moral values and a way to sort out right and wrong. Still others may simply be curious to see what the book is all about. Most of us will come to the Bible with any or all of these purposes in mind at some point over the course of our lifetimes.

No matter why or how we come to the Bible, it matters only that we come, and come regularly. As Christians we need to hear the word of God over and over, to let it soak into our minds and hearts and allow it to deepen our experience of the God revealed within its pages. One of the early monks of the Egyptian desert in the third century captured the power regular reading of the Scriptures can have in our lives:

> The nature of water is soft, the nature of stone is hard, but if a bottle is hung above a stone letting water drip down, it wears away the stone. It is like that with the word of God; it is soft and [our] heart is hard, but if [we] hear the word of God often, it will break open [our] heart to the fear of God.[1]

In the church we are seeking to know and be known by the God of the Bible. Yet how do we start to read about this God in a book so large and strange? Where do we begin? We hope this introduction to the Bible as the church's book will be the invitation to a life-long habit of reading the Scriptures, as you let your heart be shaped by the God who comes to each of us anew through these ancient and lively words.

The Bible as the Church's Book

You can tell a lot about the character of the church you are in simply by looking around you. In an Episcopal church you will see a variety of "accessories" to worship: a table or altar in prominent position at the front or center; a cross or crucifix; a pulpit from which sermons are preached; an organ or piano or other instruments to support the musical dimension of the worship, including the singing of hymns and anthems; a baptismal font. You may also see stained glass windows, often portraying stories from the Bible or church history, and perhaps a banner or painting or other kind of decoration.

You will also usually see something called a lectern: once called a reading desk, it is the usual place from which Bible passages are read aloud in the service. At one time it might have been one of the levels of an imposing "three-decker pulpit"; today lecterns vary from elaborately carved stone edifices, complete with microphone and reading lamp, to simple wooden stands. Lecterns are often molded in the shape of an eagle, the symbol of John the evangelist. No matter how grand or simple, the lectern is the place where something of great importance—something essential to the worship service—happens: the church community, gathered in worship, hears the words of its Holy Scriptures read aloud.

ENCOUNTERING THE BIBLE IN AN EPISCOPAL CHURCH

In some Episcopal churches you will find copies of the Bible available in the pews or chairs where worshipers sit, but more often there will be only the Book of Common Prayer, *The Hymnal 1982*, and perhaps other hymnbooks used for congregational singing. So it might seem that the Bible receives short shrift in Episcopal worship services, and is of lesser importance than might appear to be the case in other churches that provide copies of the Bible for use during the service. To the contrary, Episcopal services are permeated with the words, images, stories, and theologies of the Bible. Indeed, the Bible is far more central and foundational to Episcopal prayer and worship than even many Episcopalians themselves know. To see why, we need to look briefly at the prayer book that shapes the worship of the Episcopal Church, the Book of Common Prayer.[2]

The first Book of Common Prayer was largely composed by Thomas Cranmer, the Archbishop of Canterbury, and authorized for use in England in 1549. Although it was a new prayer book for a newly Protestant church, its prayers and liturgies were not written from scratch—far from it. Cranmer and his fellow revisers of the Book of Common Prayer drew from a large body of liturgical resources, both ancient and contemporary. Perhaps the most influential source was the Sarum rite in use at the cathedral in Salisbury and that spread throughout England. Some of the rites in the 1549 Prayer Book go back to the early church; others date from the early medieval period, during which the liturgies of the church were expanded and elaborated. By the mid-sixteenth century a number of prayers and services had already been translated into English from the Latin used by the Catholic Church, and Cranmer incorporated these into the new English Prayer Book as well.

The members of the English church who yearned for a prayer book in English were, of course, part of a much larger movement for reform sweeping the church. One of the fundamental tenets of this Reformation was the call for both the liturgies and the Holy Scriptures of the church to be available to the people in a language they understood, rather than the Latin known only to the clergy and the learned. After decades of fitful and individual efforts to translate various portions of the Bible in English—translations that were sometimes then forbidden, depending on the leanings of the monarchy at the time—in 1534 the English church petitioned King Henry VIII to commission the translation of the entire Bible into English. Such a royal warrant was not forthcoming, but in the following year Miles Coverdale published the first complete English Bible, nevertheless dedicated to the king, which incorporated the work of earlier translators such as William Tyndale. Although subsequent translations have long since replaced his version in Anglican worship, the beautiful Coverdale Psalter has remained in constant use and is the basis for the Psalter in our 1979 Book of Common Prayer.

Thomas Cranmer wrote the preface to one of the early revisions of the English Bible that followed in 1539/1540, known as the Great Bible, which was also largely the work of Miles Coverdale as well as other scholars of that time. These English translations were soon banned in 1546, as supporters of the classic Latin translation of the Bible, the Vulgate, regained a political foothold in those tumultuous times, but under Edward VI use of the English Bible was allowed once again.

We see this Reformation concern for the Bible to be available to the people in a language they understood in one of the prayers of Cranmer, composed for the 1549 Book of Common Prayer:

> Blessed lord, which hast caused all holy Scriptures to bee written for our learnyng; graunte us that we maye in suche wise heare them, read, marke, learne, and inwardly digeste them; that by pacience, and coumfort of thy holy woorde, we may embrace, and ever holde fast the blessed hope of everlasting life, which thou hast geven us in our saviour Jesus Christe.

In the 1979 Book of Common Prayer we read this collect (a prayer that "collects" the themes or images of the day or event) near the end of the Season after Pentecost, just before the beginning of Advent. But this collect was originally associated with the second Sunday in Advent, and foreshadows part of the reading from the epistle to the Romans that would also have been heard at worship services on that day: "Whatsoever thinges are written aforetime, they are written for our learning, that we through pacience, and comfort of the scriptures, might have hope" (Romans 15:4).

The collect not only highlights the value the reformers placed on the reading of Scripture, but also is a good example of the way in which the words and images of the Bible are seamlessly intertwined with prayers and liturgies in Anglican prayer books. One of the liturgical scholars responsible for our 1979 Prayer Book, Marion J. Hatchett, notes that the rather pointed use of the word "all" in the phrase "who caused *all* holy Scriptures to be written for our learning" recalls Cranmer's criticism in the first Prayer Book's preface regarding the late medieval church's practice of keeping so many saints' days that the reading of the books of the Bible in course was constantly interrupted. Cranmer made sure that in the 1549 Prayer Book almost the entire Bible was read in an orderly arrangement during the course of each year in the Daily Office.[3]

Cranmer likewise placed the "Table and Kalendar for Psalms and Lessons, with necessary rules pertaining to the same" at the very beginning of the Book of Common Prayer, just after the preface. He noted that during the services of Matins (Morning Prayer) and Evensong (Evening Prayer), the Old Testament "shall be read through every year once, except certain books and chapters, which be least edifying, and might best be spared" (such as chapters listing genealogies—Genesis 10, for example—and large parts of Leviticus). The New Testament, except for the book of Revelation, would be read three times each year. Thus from the time of the Reformation, Anglicans heard the stories and words of the Bible in the language they understood, as part and parcel of their prayer and worship.

Those of us who joined the Episcopal Church after 1979 may not be aware that in previous prayer books the texts of the Scripture readings for the Sunday liturgy were actually included in full. Today we have only the references to which readings occur on a certain Sunday or holy day, and instead the passages are read from a Bible or book of lectionary texts. When Cranmer first wrote the Book of Common Prayer, however, Bibles were not as abundantly available as they are now, and it was the custom in medieval prayer books and missals to print the Scripture lessons within the services themselves. Thus these earlier prayer books were more of a "combination book" of prayers and selections from the Bible, and perhaps this format made the scriptural foundations of Anglican worship more obvious. We can still recognize the words, images, and theology of the Bible in our prayers and services, and they become even more readily apparent when we come to know the Bible better. The words and images of the Bible are absolutely central to each liturgy in the 1979 Book of Common Prayer; indeed, we might go so far as to say that the services of the Prayer Book are simply a way of praying the Bible, day by day. Episcopalians who participate in the church's worship and prayer regularly will thus come to know the words and images of the Bible very well indeed, perhaps by heart.

We might enjoy hearing these distant echoes in our liturgies, yet if we do not know the Bible itself well enough to recognize their source, then we miss much of their depth and richness of meaning. As beautiful or haunting or compelling as these words may be, they may also seem to be simply the words of people from a different time and place. How do we who pray the words of Scripture in our liturgies come to speak those words as *our* words, come to know the biblical story as *our* story?

THE BIBLE'S STORY, OUR STORY

At the heart of the Bible is the story of God's people and their ongoing relationship with the God who created them, invited them into relationship, saved them, and forgave them. Within this larger story are hundreds of stories of individuals, rulers, prophets, disciples, and philosophers. And for Christians, at its very core is the story of the Messiah (from Greek, *Christ*), who is Jesus, the Incarnation ("in the flesh") of God.

Many of the stories of the Bible are skillfully and beautifully told, with the power to arouse in us a yearning to know the God of whom they speak. But at the same time these stories are very old, and it might seem that we need stories from a more contemporary time to describe our vision of God and God's relationship with the human race. And, as it happens, we *do* tell those stories as well. In the church we are continually seeking to bring together the old stories of the Bible—the foundation of our faith—with our own encounters and perceptions of God in the world around us.

This dialogue between Scripture and our lives today takes many forms. It may happen in a formal way in the worship of the church, as preachers and listeners wrestle with the day's readings from the Bible and the wisdom they offer for contemporary life. It may come about in works of fiction, as in the stories of Flannery O'Conner or Frederick Buechner, as these authors create contemporary characters who embody the biblical encounter with God. The dialogue may develop in a Bible study or discussion group, as people tell their stories of an emerging faith and connect them with the stories told in the Bible. Or it may occur as a scientist or historian or theologian seeks to interpret the teachings of Scripture in a way that makes sense for us today. In all of these conversations between the stories of the Bible and the stories we live today, the Bible is a touchstone or compass that continually helps us to orient ourselves to the God who is revealed in the biblical stories, as well as to discover in the events of our lives the presence and activity of that God.

The Bible is a living book. While the written text of the Christian Scriptures was formally set during the first three centuries after Jesus lived and died, the interpretation of the texts and their connections to the particular concerns of each era of history continues. The Apostles' and Nicene Creeds, for example, were an attempt to render the teachings of Scripture in ways of thought that were very familiar to the Greek and Roman Christians who recited them. Each age, in some sense, tells the Bible's story over again; yet we retain the original and foundational stories because taken as a whole they have a certain kind of completeness.

Just as none of the books of the Bible tells the whole story (even the story of Jesus is told in four different ways) and just as it took many centuries for the whole story to be told, so each age of human history tells its own portion of the story. But each age must also have the *rest* of the story if it is to understand and embrace the truth about the God who is revealed in the Bible. Indeed, many people over the centuries have considered the finalization of the list of writings included in the canon of Scripture during the fourth and fifth centuries a tragic event, for such a closing of the canon implies that the revelation of God in human history ended with the era of the apostles. Ralph Waldo Emerson used the phrase "not spake but speaketh" to convey his belief that the revelation of God to human beings did not cease when the limits of the Bible were set. Does God no longer speak to and through the human race? What if we were told that the letters we write, the stories we tell, the sermons we preach, the histories we compile, the prayers we pray, the hymns we sing might one day become part of the canon of Christian Scripture describing the activity and presence of God among us now? How would we live our faith differently? How would our views of the stories of the Bible change?

There are, of course, passages in the Bible that are difficult for those of us living in the contemporary world to understand or embrace. The depiction of God in the early history of Israel as a warrior deity who destroys enemies and demands that entire cities and nations be utterly eliminated seems to challenge the Christian understanding of a loving God. The descriptions of relationships between husband and wife found in both the Old and New Testaments are radically different from our contemporary understanding of marriage. There are laws about eating and financial arrangements that are not part of our culture and economy—nor would we want them to be. The source of many of the ongoing struggles in the church today is this difficult issue of how Christians come to terms with the idea that Holy Scripture tells us the truth about God while offering us images and demands that are in conflict with the ways we live and relate to God today. We will look more closely at some of these difficult issues in chapters three and four, which focus on the interpretation of the Bible.

While our varying interpretations of the Bible can be a source of conflict among Christians, studying the Bible with other people can also offer the great reward of learning how God works in different and varied ways with God's different and varied people. Such study helps us to see that while the Bible tells stories about people and situations from long ago, it is also telling *our* story. We find in the Bible's stories of struggle, discovery, failure, joy, discouragement, and hope reflections of our own stories of similar experiences.

In fact, the Scriptures are quite explicit about this connection. As the stories of the ancient people of Israel are told, especially the story of the Exodus (the escape of the Israelites from slavery in Egypt and their journey to the promised land), the Bible declares that this is not just about "them": it is also about "us." Israelites of many generations have connected themselves to the Exodus experience by reciting a passage from Deuteronomy as applying to their own lives:

> You shall make this response before the LORD your God: "A wandering Aramean was my ancestor; he went down into Egypt and lived there as an alien, few in number, and there he became a great nation, mighty and populous. When the Egyptians treated us harshly and afflicted us, by imposing hard labor on us, we cried to the LORD, the God of our ancestors; the LORD heard our voice and saw our affliction, our toil, and our oppression. The LORD brought us out of Egypt with a mighty hand and an outstretched arm, with a terrifying display of power, and with signs and wonders; and he brought us into this place and gave us this land, a land flowing with milk and honey." (Deuteronomy 26:5–9)

In much the same way, for Christians the story of the Scriptures is also *our* story of salvation, and a way through which we are invited to share in the work of God in the world. The Israelites' story of freedom from slavery in Egypt becomes our Christian story, as we experience freedom from slavery to sin through our relationship with Christ. We gather as a community in worship and praise to tell and retell these stories in celebration and remembrance. The Jewish community knows this immediacy in their Passover celebrations. Likewise, for Christians, while the liturgy of the Holy Eucharist can seem to be merely describing events in the life of Jesus in Jerusalem long ago, it is actually a way of experiencing those events in the present, as we take upon ourselves the story of salvation today in the presence of Christ. As we make the connections between the biblical story and the events of our lives as people of faith in the twenty-first century, we come to understand in new ways that the story of the Bible is indeed *our* story.

WHY READ THE BIBLE?

If we understand the Bible in this way, not just as the stories of people who believed in God many years ago or of events that happened long before any of us were born, but our own stories about a common faith in the same God, then we can see why the Bible has long held, and still commands, a central place in the church's work and worship. It is our family history; it tells us who we are. It is the sourcebook and guide for all we do today, just as it was the sourcebook and guide for all that God did for those who went before us. We look to the Bible for a sense of how we are to live and what our vocation (our work) in the world is to be. We also look to the Bible to help us comprehend how much God has done for us, so that our life and work is a response of gratitude for God's gift of steadfast and long-suffering love for all of creation, not a duty based upon what we perceive to be God's demands.

We read the Bible as Christians because it is so central to our faith in God. Sometimes we read it together, during our services of worship and prayer, so that we hear its stories as a community and can reflect upon it using a common language. We also read it in church so that we all hear a large portion of the Bible over a certain period of time. Left to our own devices we might pick and choose the stories we read, but we need to hear not just the parts of Scripture that are familiar, comforting, and pleasing, but also those that we do not know well, those that trouble or disturb us. By hearing God's word in all of its variety we can draw from it the insights and teachings that can challenge and comfort us in our daily life. Reading the Bible in the context of worship and prayer draws us to respond to that challenge and empowers us to put the message of the Bible to work in our daily lives.

We also read the Bible privately, in our times of personal prayer, study, and meditation. Here we are listening to how God speaks to us individually, and how the words of Scripture draw us into the conversation of the church about the work of Christians in the world. As we read we may also be doing our own theological reflection on God and God's relationship to our world, as well as our personal way of living. Personal reading may help us see more clearly what it means for each of us to respond to God's invitation to relationship as described in the Bible, and may invite us to think about our way of life—morally, economically, politically, socially—in ways that invite us into new and "holier" ways of life.

Finally, studying the Bible in small groups is also a way of deepening and expanding our knowledge of the Scriptures. In groups we are encouraged to hear other people's understandings and perceptions, and to learn from their knowledge and expertise. In groups we can try out our interpretations and responses to what the Bible seems to be saying, both to understand why others agree or disagree, and to find support for the ways the Scriptures invite us to change. The record of the church's history makes it painfully clear that it is easy to misinterpret the words of the Bible, based on misunderstandings of who God is and what God asks of us, so the wise counsel and corrective influence of other Christians is an essential part of growing in faith.

In response to a question about whether Jesus was someone worth bothering to meet, the disciple Philip said simply, "Come and see" (John 1:46). That too is the invitation of the Bible: "Come and see." Come and learn who God is, come and hear God's word, come and change the direction in which your life is going, come and be forgiven, come and be part of the community called to be God's people in the world. It can seem a daunting invitation. But remember that you have the support and encouragement of others as you open the pages of this big, intimidating book and begin to see how the message of the Bible can be of value to you.

QUESTIONS FOR REFLECTION AND DISCUSSION

1. What was your relationship with the Bible as a child or teenager? What is your relationship with the Bible now? How do you understand its place in your life?

2. Have you tried to read the Bible before? What has made it difficult? What would you need to make it easier for you to read the Bible with some understanding? Can you think of parts of the Bible that are easier for you to read?

3. Think about the place of the Bible in the life of your congregation. Are there Bibles available in the pews? In the church library? How is the Bible read and interpreted in your worship services? Do people in the congregation gather for Bible study?

4. How would you write a letter to a friend or community describing your experience of God, or a gospel telling the story of Jesus? How have you seen Jesus in your world? What words or images would you use? How does the Bible's story reflect your experience? How is it different?

What Is the Bible?

If you were to visit the worship services of a number of different Christian churches, you would encounter a fascinating if sometimes confusing variety of hymns, prayers, orders of service, and styles of worship. Regardless of which congregation you visit or what the focus of the service might be, however, in every church you would hear some portion of the Bible read aloud. In some churches you would hear many passages taken from a number of books of the Bible; in others, you might hear only a few verses from a single book. Yet the common bond between all the varieties of Christian worship is the practice of reading aloud the texts we call the Bible.

For the church the Bible is the source of God's word and the revelation of truth, yet perhaps the most defining aspect of a church or denomination is its particular interpretation of that word of God. Although the Bible is central to the church's life and worship, the structures erected on that foundation can be so different as to seem completely detached from one another. So what exactly *is* this book that means so much to the church, this book that evokes devotion and confirms faith in so many, and yet is also the source of much confusion, controversy, and division?

What Do We Mean by "Scripture"?

Most of the religions of the world have some form of sacred writings that describe the beliefs and experiences of that religious community, and are held to contain a particular revelation of who God is and how God acts in human history. Christians most often use the word "Bible" to describe their sacred writings, and while this is the most familiar term, these texts actually have a number of names. The term "Bible" comes from the Greek word *biblia*, which means "little books." It was the word used by the writers of the Greek version of the Hebrew Scriptures (the Septuagint) when they spoke of the "books" of the Law, or the "books" of the Prophets. When the word was later translated into Latin after the many "little books" had been compiled into a single book, it became the singular *Scriptura*—and you will still hear the Bible referred to as both "the Scriptures" and "Scripture" today.

In the church you will often hear the Bible referred to in other ways as well. It is sometimes called the word of God, and often the word "Holy" is added to its title—the Holy Bible, the Holy Scriptures. It may be called the Book, the Message, or simply the Word. For Martin Luther, the word "Scripture" referred to the Old Testament, while the books of the New Testament were better called "proclamation" or "message," for he noted that Jesus did not command his disciples to write books, but to *proclaim* the gospel. Thus for Christians these names for the texts of the Bible are in many ways interchangeable, though they may also reflect the stance of a particular faith group toward the Bible. These various names reflect the long history of the church's reading and study of these texts, and the different strands of Christian tradition that have developed over the past two thousand years.

The books of the Bible were not written at the same time, or by the same person—far from it. Rather, these texts were recorded from the oral traditions of the people who told their stories about God and God's involvement in human history over and over, from generation to generation, for centuries. Even after the texts were written down they remained fluid for a surprisingly long time: because they were copied by hand the errors, comments, and changes introduced by the scribes entered into the scriptural record as well. It was common practice to destroy or reuse the old parchments, so we have few of the ancient manuscripts to which we can compare these copies. This fluidity of a written text can be a difficult concept to grasp for those of us who are accustomed to modern methods of publishing. If we buy a certain book in a bookstore in Chicago we expect it to be exactly the same book that is on the shelves in London. And we expect it to be written by exactly the same person whose name appears as the author on the cover.

Similarly, if we go to that bookstore in Chicago or London and purchase a Bible, the words of each Bible will be exactly the same, if we choose the same translation. But the Bible was not originally written that way: the stories were passed down through oral tradition for centuries, recorded and copied and edited and adapted for centuries more, and only relatively recently, with the invention of the printing press, solidified into a printed set of texts that no longer change. Moreover, a single author did not write most of the books of the Bible, nor do the names attributed to the books of the Bible necessarily reflect the actual author or authors. It was customary at the time to attach the name of a well-known authority or teacher, such as Moses or David or Paul, to writings that were believed to reflect that person's thoughts or teachings.

Another concept that is difficult for us to grasp today is the idea that an oral tradition could be passed down as dependably as written texts. Evidently our ancestors were much more adept at memorizing long passages and stories than we are, and they trusted the stories told and retold through the generations more than we are apt to do. In the fourth century, for example, Bishop Cyril of Jerusalem urged his baptismal candidates to "commit to memory" the Christian creed that was used for baptism in his diocese, and "to rehearse it with all diligence among yourselves, *not writing it out on paper*, but engraving it by the memory upon your heart."[4] In that time of persecution the most urgent reason behind his avoidance of a written record was the fear that the "mysteries" of the Christian faith would fall into Roman hands and be used against the community of the faithful. But in Bishop Cyril's episcopal directive we see his confidence in the words of the creed being preserved and passed on to the next generation of Christians through the memorization and repeated telling and retelling of the creed among believers.

THE DEVELOPMENT OF THE CANON

The Bible, as we know it, has a fixed form. That form evolved over several years into the collection of writings that we know as the Hebrew Scriptures (or Old Testament) and the Christian Scriptures (or New Testament). These fixed writings are called the canon of Scripture because they were formally set for Christians by a canon law in the seventh century CE.

We do not know exactly when the books that recorded the stories that had been handed down for generations and that later became the Hebrew Scriptures were collected and written. These texts were probably written in Hebrew quite early in the history of Israel, perhaps between about 1000 and 300 BCE, but they were not gathered into an unchanging list or canon until quite late—about 90 to 120 CE, after the Jewish temple had been destroyed and the Jewish community felt a need to gather their sacred books together in a single collection with greater uniformity. These books are divided into three main sections: The Law (Torah), which are the first five books from Genesis to Deuteronomy; The Prophets (Nebi'im), which includes the historical records of Joshua, Judges, Samuel, and Kings as well as the prophetic books of Isaiah, Jeremiah, and the other prophets; and The Writings (Ketubim), which includes the well-known books of Psalms, Job, and Proverbs. The Hebrew Scriptures are known in Judaism as the *Tanak* or *Tanakh*, which is simply an acronym of the first letters of Torah, Nebi'im, and Ketubim.

A Greek translation of the Hebrew texts, known as the Septuagint (the Latin word for seventy, based on the legendary number of the translators), began around 250 BCE in Alexandria and continued for perhaps a century or more. A Greek translation of the Hebrew Scriptures was needed by that time because many if not most of the Jews of the Diaspora—those scattered throughout the Greek world—could no longer read or understand Hebrew. If the presence for several centuries of a vigorous Jewish community of faith and scholarly learning in Alexandria following the translation of the Septuagint is any indication, then the effort to have the stories and history of the people of Israel available in the language of the people was indeed effective.

The translation of the Hebrew Scriptures into Greek opened the way not only for Greek-speaking Jews to hear and read the story of the God of Israel, but for vast numbers of Gentiles to as well. With the Septuagint the Hebrew Bible became accessible to the literate world as never before. The Septuagint is also of critical importance to Christians, for it was this translation that was used by the early Christian church. Indeed, for the most part Christians would rely solely on this Greek translation for over a thousand years, and it therefore played a pivotal role in the development of Christian beliefs and worship.

Perhaps the most famous example of its influence on Christian theology is the translation of the Hebrew word for "young woman" with the Greek word for "virgin" in the book of the prophet Isaiah (7:14). This text thus supported the belief in the virginal conception of Jesus described in the Greek New Testament (see Matthew 1:18–25)—a belief that also made its way into the Qu'ran for Muslims (Sura III:47). Thus the ongoing formation and interpretation of the Hebrew Scriptures within the Jewish community was to play an integral role in the first-century offshoot of Judaism, the Christian church.

The books and letters that were to form the New Testament were written in Greek, with a few words in Aramaic, the dialect of Hebrew that was in use during the first century CE, somewhere between about 45 and 120. The earliest of these Christian writings were the letters from the apostles and other Christian leaders to the congregations in cities like Corinth and Ephesus scattered throughout the Middle East and the Roman Empire. These were practical letters filled with advice and admonition to the very new Christian communities who were attempting to live out the gospel of Jesus Christ in diverse and often hostile environments. These letters were circulated among the churches and read aloud when the community would gather for worship or study, perhaps much as we read them in our worship services today.

Soon accounts of the life and teachings of Jesus began to be written down—not as historical documents, but as records that bore witness to the Christian faith in Jesus as the Messiah (in Greek, "the Christ") and as the Son of God. A number of gospel accounts were written, including the four that were eventually included in our New Testament; these seem to be the first books that were considered to be authoritative scriptural accounts that supplemented the record of the Old Testament. The writer of the gospel of Luke also wrote the Acts of the Apostles, in which he describes the formation of the early church, especially the life of the most prolific writer of letters in the New Testament, the apostle Paul. The last book of the New Testament, the Revelation to John or the Apocalypse, is part of a large body of apocalyptic ("end of time") literature common at that time.

Over time, the Christian churches began to feel the need to collect these writings into a single book and to distinguish between the writings that were "orthodox" and those that were considered "heterodox" or "heretical," or perhaps reflected the beliefs of a particular Christian community or sect but not those of the broader church as a whole. We have a list of the writings that were being read in the church in Rome at the turn of the third century, and these books include the four canonical gospels as well as many of the letters that appear in our New Testament today. Other writings, such as the letter to the Hebrews, 2 Peter, Jude, 2 and 3 John, and Revelation, were not universally acknowledged as authoritative and their place in the Christian Scriptures was disputed among the various Christian communities.

From the writings of two leading bishops in the early church, the historian Eusebius of Caesarea and Athanasius of Alexandria, we can see that by the middle of the fourth century the contents of the New Testament as we know it today had gained wide acceptance among the churches; in fact, a list of these canonical books appears for the first time in a letter of Athanasius from 367 CE. The various church communities continued to debate the inclusion of some of the letters, especially James, 1 Peter, and 1 John, for some time to come, but at a church council in 692 CE the process of forming the canon of the New Testament was formally closed.

MAJOR SECTIONS OF THE CHRISTIAN BIBLE

For Christians, there are two major sections of the Bible: the Hebrew Scriptures (frequently called the Old Testament by Christians) and the Christian Scriptures (the New Testament). Verna Dozier reminds us of the multiplicity of books in the Christian Bible in her classic book *The Dream of God*:

> The Bible is not a book; that very name is a misnomer. It is a library of sixty-six books and it is arranged like a library into law books, the Torah, followed by history books, then literature—hymns and poetry and drama and aphorisms and philosophy—then prophetic works. The New Testament has a similar arrangement: gospels, then history, letters, and finally an apocalypse.[5]

In this library called the Bible, the Hebrew Scriptures comprise the first thirty-nine books, while the writings of the early Christians comprise the last twenty-seven. In many Bibles, especially those used by Roman Catholics and Episcopalians, there is a third section: fifteen books called the Apocrypha. These are additional books from the Hebrew people's sacred story, like Ecclesiasticus and 1 and 2 Maccabees, that were included only in the Greek Septuagint and were therefore considered less authoritative by Jewish scholars and rabbis.

Thus we encounter two religious traditions in the Bible: Jewish and Christian. In the early years of the Christian movement, Christians thought of themselves as a part of the Jewish religious tradition; the Hebrew Scriptures were their Bible. Furthermore, they believed Jesus was actually the fulfillment of all that had been spoken of and promised in the books of the Law and the Prophets; he was the embodiment of the Messiah who was to come and save God's people. Because they held that in Jesus the promises of God had been fulfilled, they began to call the Hebrew Scriptures the "Old Testament" and Christian writings the "New Testament," describing the new covenant that God had made with humankind in the life, death, and resurrection of Jesus.

In time, it was not possible to maintain this connection between the emerging Christian teachings and the traditions of Judaism. As the two faiths separated, most Christians continued to believe that God had been revealed in the Hebrew Scriptures as well as the Christian writings, and that Jesus was the fulfillment of the Old Testament's teachings. There were some, however, who believed the Hebrew Scriptures no longer had a place in the Christian Bible. They were led by an influential Christian named Marcion, who came to Rome in 140 CE and established congregations that developed their own list of canonical Scriptures, which did not include the Hebrew Scriptures and even excluded many of the commonly circulated letters and three of the four gospels that would become part of the New Testament. Marcion's attempt to develop his own canon helped spur other church leaders to decide which books should be authoritative for Christians, and thus encouraged the development of the Bible as a permanent collection of books. Their decision to include the Hebrew Scriptures in the Christian canon meant that Christians retained the Jewish tradition as an important part of their religious heritage.

The Literature of the Bible

As we have seen, the Bible is not like most books, which are written by a single author or compiled by a single editor. Rather, it is more like a library: it contains a wide variety of literature written by many different people and material gathered throughout centuries of human history. The two major sections of the Bible tell God's story from different eras and different perspectives, and within each division are many varieties of literature, from folk stories to poems to letters. Sometimes these literary forms are clearly identifiable and easy to recognize (as, for example, in the letters of Paul). But in many books of the Bible they are mixed together in ways that readers can find confusing (as in the prophet Jeremiah's book, where there is a mixture of history, prose, and poetry). Older versions of the Bible tended to print the text in a continuous, prose-like form. The newer versions and translations make a clearer distinction between poetry, prose, and other literary forms.

When we read a novel, we know it is a story of fiction that offers an insight into the human condition in some way; when we study books of history or philosophy, we will look for a different sort of human knowledge. Poets, theologians, historians, political pundits, prophets—all approach their subjects in a different way, and we need to understand the purpose and style of their writing in order to understand what they are trying to say. Likewise, when we read the books of the Bible it is important to know what kind of literature we are reading. Just knowing some of the hallmarks and telltale signs of the various forms of literature and their use in the biblical narrative helps us to understand the Bible more fully and as it was intended to be heard.

The Hebrew Scriptures

We find the greatest variety of writings in the Hebrew Scriptures. In the very first book, for example, we are confronted with several different kinds of literature. In the opening chapters of Genesis we are given the "myth of creation." Perhaps we ought to say two myths of creation, since the first two chapters are a blending of two creation stories, one about the seven-day work of God, the other about the creation of human beings and their rebellion against God's way. A *myth* is a story that seems to be about something that actually took place. As Frederick Buechner writes:

> The raw material of a myth, like the raw material of a dream, may be something that actually happened once. But myths, like dreams, do not tell us much about that kind of actuality. The creation of man, Adam and Eve, the Tower of Babel, Oedipus—they do not tell us primarily about events. They tell us about ourselves. In popular usage, a myth has come to mean a story that is not true. Historically speaking that may well be so. Humanly speaking, a myth is a story that is always true.[6]

In other words, myth is a way to express a culture's view of the world, or to explain a religious or cultural practice or belief.

Similarly, we find several *legends*—or portions of legends—in the next few chapters of Genesis. The story of Noah is a legendary tale. While myths tell us about cultural concepts and circumstances, legends and sagas tell about the people who were important in the early formation of the society. They are often depicted as "heroes," exemplary models of what it is to be a great human being. Noah is said to "have found favor in God's sight." So, the story of his salvation and his preservation of the creation marks an important turning point in the Genesis story.

Genesis continues with the story of Abram (who becomes Abraham) and his family. This portion of Genesis is a *saga*, filled with legendary features. Abraham is a model of faith and obedience. The stories of his journeys, his struggles with marriage and family, his ritual life, while perhaps rooted in a historical life, mark him as a model for Israel and the exemplary human being. This saga continues with the stories of Abraham's offspring, Isaac, Jacob, and the twelve sons of Jacob, especially Joseph.

One of the distinguishing marks of the Hebrew legends, however, is their realism. While the legendary characters had profound faith in and devotion to the God of Israel, they also reveal flaws. Throughout the legends of Hebrew history we see that the giants of Israelite history (including Moses, David, and Elijah) were people of tremendous faith and courage, but were also human beings who had weaknesses and who made serious mistakes.

Myths and legends are part of every culture; they are part of the formative history of every nation and people. In the Hebrew Scriptures, these kinds of literature appear not only in Genesis but also in the *historical* books, like Samuel and Kings. Some scholars refer to them as the "pre-history" of Israel—the time so far back in the memory of the people that there are no written records of the events. Others suggest that their purpose is to set a tone for the culture and to establish a theological perspective about humans and their relationship to God.

In fact, as we read the historical books of the Bible that describe the acts of kings and various officials of Judah and Israel, we discover that the events are chosen and portrayed in such a way as not merely to relate facts, but to point to the relationship between God and the nations and to interpret the meaning of key events. In other words, the books of the Hebrew Scriptures were written to bear witness to the faith of the people of Israel in their God, not as historical documents as we would understand that term. There may be some genuine history in the Bible, but it is not always clear just how accurate it is, because the writers and editors were always seeking to find in the events of any given time the quality and consequences of the behavior of people and the responses of God and God's relationship with them.

Many figures in the story of the Hebrew people (such as David and some of the other kings) have been identified in discoveries by archaeologists, although the particular stories about them cannot be verified. We know that the writers of the Bible conveyed information about their history not merely because it was interesting to them, but because they believed that God was to be known and understood through those events.

Other parts of the Bible that often confuse and defeat readers are the *genealogies*. In Genesis these lists of names interrupt the flow of the narrative in several places (such as the naming of Adam's descendants in Genesis 5, and the list of Jesus' forebears in Matthew 1), and to us seem unnecessary and incidental to the text. While we do not know all the reasons for the inclusion of these lists of generations, it seems that there are at least two possible explanations. First, they help establish a timeline for the story, which is measured not in years, but in "generations." Second, they help to maintain the integrity of the nation of Israel by keeping all of their ancestors as a part of the story. Ancestry was important in Israel, especially after Abraham, because the nation thought of itself as a chosen "race" of people, based on their descent from Abraham. At various times in the history of Israel, marriage outside the group was prohibited. So, while many readers today simply skip over the genealogies to get on with the story and few church lectionaries include them for reading aloud in worship services, for the people writing and compiling the sacred texts, these names were an important part of their heritage.

Some of the oldest passages in the Bible are *poetic*. The Song of Deborah in the book of Judges is said to be a very ancient poem, probably remembered and passed down through the oral traditions of the people. Poetry plays an important role in the Hebrew Scriptures, in several different ways. First, poems and songs are often an interpretive insertion in a story that is mostly action—a way for us to know what the theological or social significance of the event is. For example, in the first book of Samuel, the poem known as the Song of Hannah is inserted in the story of Samuel's conception and birth and interprets the significance of that birth for the reader (2:1–10).

Poetry is also a means by which God is often addressed directly, and by which God often addresses the people. In the book of Psalms, for example, there are one hundred fifty poems that address God in various ways. Many were written as liturgical prayers and songs used in Jewish worship, much like the texts of hymns and the prayers we use in our church services. Some of the Psalms are songs of thanksgiving and joy; others are songs of lament and fear. Some were composed for special days of worship; others for more secular occasions, like the enthronement of a new king. Some are very familiar and comforting to us, such as the Twenty-third Psalm, while others are more troubling and seem quite foreign to our vision of God, like the portions of Psalm 137 that call for revenge and the dashing of the enemy's little ones against a rock.

Poetry is also used in the Hebrew Scriptures to convey the words of God to the people. Jeremiah, Isaiah, and other prophets of Israel used poetry much of the time as they reported to the people, "Thus says the Lord." *Prophecy* is a form of communication that we rarely hear—or at least recognize as such—today. While we think of "prophets" as those who predict future events, the primary work of the prophets of Israel was to convey and interpret the word of God to the nation. Since the nations of Israel and Judah were theocracies (nations where their God was considered the primary ruler), it was important to have a means to know what God wanted. This was especially the case when the official religious spokespersons—the priests and Levites and false prophets—were not trustworthy. Although in early Israel the king was expected to be the mediator between God and the people, as time went on the kings became arrogant and corrupt and of questionable faith. Prophets like Amos and Hosea came forward claiming to speak for God and to lead the people back to righteousness. Their words are both critical of many of the religious and social practices of their times and consoling, reminding people of the loving kindness of their God even as they challenged Israel to return to God's laws. As these prophets experienced rejection and ridicule and became aware of the stubbornness of kings and people, they began to give warnings of God's impending punishment for their disobedience—the destruction of the nation. Since these warnings turned out to be correct, they became the source of the idea that prophets make predictions. In the years that followed the destruction of Jerusalem around 586 BCE, prophets of the exile like Ezekiel became important sources of the renewal of the religion of Israel.

We also find *parables* in the Old Testament. Parables are familiar to many Christians because they are a form of storytelling Jesus used frequently in his teachings. These stories seem to be about one thing, but are actually about God's relationship with God's people. For example, in the book of the prophet Isaiah we find a parable in which the nation of Israel is described as God's vineyard:

> Let me sing for my beloved my love-song concerning his vineyard: My beloved had a vineyard on a very fertile hill. He dug it and cleared it of stones, and planted it with choice vines; he built a watchtower in the midst of it, and hewed out a wine vat in it; he expected it to yield grapes, but it yielded wild grapes. And now, inhabitants of Jerusalem and people of Judah, judge between me and my vineyard. What more was there to do for my vineyard that I have not done in it? When I expected it to yield grapes, why did it yield wild grapes?

The parable goes on to include Isaiah's prophecy of the destruction of the nation, spoken in the words of God:

> And now I will tell you what I will do to my vineyard. I will remove its hedge, and it shall be devoured; I will break down its wall, and it shall be trampled down. I will make it a waste; it shall not be pruned or hoed, and it shall be overgrown with briers and thorns.

And, as in many parables, Isaiah concludes his story of the vineyard with keys to its interpretation:

> For the vineyard of the LORD of hosts is the house of Israel, and the people of Judah are his pleasant planting; he expected justice, but saw bloodshed; righteousness, but heard a cry! (Isaiah 5:1–7)

In the years following the exile of the people of Israel (586–537 BCE), several new forms of literature began to appear in the Hebrew Scriptures, as Jews living in Babylon and other non-Jewish nations were exposed to other kinds of writings. Some of these forms of literature became the media in which Jewish writers expressed their faith in God. One such form is known as the *Wisdom* literature. It shares with Greek and other Mediterranean cultures an interest in speculation about God and the world. In many ways it is a form of philosophy, although in the hands of the Hebrew writers it always had a theological—or God-centered—emphasis. Two examples of Wisdom literature in the Hebrew Scriptures are the book of Ecclesiastes, which is a meditation on the frailty and difficulty of human existence, and the book of Proverbs, a series of practical sayings for various groups and situations.

The *apocalyptic* writings are another new form of literature that grew out of Israel's experience in exile. Apocalyptic writings deal with the end of time, or with the fulfillment of God's purposes for human beings. They often contain vivid dreams and visions of heavenly beings who are struggling against the forces of evil on God's behalf and who exemplify faithful devotion to God and God's ways. After their return to the land of Israel and the city of Jerusalem following the exile, the Israelites had no independent government, but lived under the domination of foreign powers. They began to think that God's "plan" would one day avenge their suffering and restore the kingdom of David by a mighty supernatural act. This future hope for deliverance and restoration forms the basis of most of the apocalyptic writings. The book of Daniel and the book of Zechariah both contain apocalyptic sections.

Within the books of the Hebrew Scriptures, especially the writings of the prophets, there is often a confusing mixture of these various kinds of literature. A narration about a particular event may suddenly turn into a poetic outburst; a parable may be housed in the midst of several poetic stanzas. It is apparent that over the centuries a good deal of editing has been done with the texts that comprise the books of the Hebrew Scriptures, and the editors have chosen to string together a variety of materials, perhaps based on a sense of their relationship to specific events or people.

All of this literature may seem to make the reading of the Hebrew Scriptures rather daunting. For those of us who are just beginning to explore the books of the Hebrew Scriptures, it may be helpful to read them from a study Bible or translation, such as the New English Bible, that divides the text into sections with a caption to alert the reader to the points where the subject or situation changes. It is also good to keep a commentary or two handy—both Christian and Jewish. Knowing about the various kinds of literature you will encounter in the books of the Hebrew Scriptures and keeping an eye open for the shifts and changes in the text can make the reading of these complex and challenging writings much more interesting.

The Christian Scriptures

When we turn to the Christian Scriptures, we find many of the same kinds of literature. This is not unexpected, since the Christian writers considered the Hebrew Scriptures their Bible, just as we do. They were very familiar with and made extensive use of the texts of the Hebrew Scriptures, quoting poetry and psalms, referring to important characters and sagas, identifying prophecies they believed were fulfilled in the life and death of Jesus. But in the Christian Scriptures we also have several new and different forms of literature than we encountered in the Hebrew texts.

Because the books of the Christian Scriptures were written over a period of perhaps only a hundred years, their consistency and uniformity is greater than that of the Hebrew Scriptures. They were written in Greek, so they have a somewhat different "feel" than the Hebrew writings. Hebrew is a verb-dependent language, expressing its thoughts and ideas in action words. The Greek language is more philosophical and rational, using abstract images and words. While stories dominate the Hebrew Scriptures, we will see that only one story dominates the Christian writings: the story of Jesus and the growth of the new Christian communities following his resurrection. Just as the stories of Israel were retold in poetry, song, and parable, the story of Jesus is also examined in more subtle and reflective ways.

The story of Jesus is told in the New Testament in the books called *gospels*. (The word "gospel"—literally *God's spiel*—is an English rendering of the Greek word for "good news.") These four books—Matthew, Mark, Luke, and John—tell the story of Jesus in four similar yet distinct ways. A gospel is a genre unique to the Christian writings. While it outlines events in the life of Jesus, a gospel is not a biography of Jesus in the modern sense of a "life story." Instead, its primary concern is to convey the writer's belief about who Jesus was and is. John, for example, notes that he wrote his gospel "so that you may come to believe that Jesus is the Messiah, the Son of God, and that through believing you may have life in his name" (John 20:31). Mark likewise opens his gospel with a declaration of belief: "The beginning of the good news [or gospel] of Jesus Christ, the Son of God." Mark tells us right away that this story is not about any normal human being, but about the Son of God. Mark selected events in Jesus' life and recorded accounts of what Jesus said and taught in order to convey that message of faith.

Each of the gospels shares a common outline of Jesus' life, beginning in Galilee, moving to Jerusalem, and culminating in his arrest, trial, death, and resurrection. Each gospel, however, tells the story from different perspectives and in different ways, though often using similar events and sayings. Matthew, Mark, and Luke (often called "synoptic," meaning "seen together") share much in common. Many biblical scholars today believe that Mark was written first and that both Matthew and Luke used his gospel as a basis for theirs, while still adding new material to Mark's sparing account. Luke focuses on Jesus as a healer and friend of the outcast; Matthew portrays him as a teacher and rabbi; for Mark, Jesus proclaimed the message of a kingdom of God that was immediate and urgent. John presents still another Jesus—the Logos, or Word of God, often speaking through mysteries and riddles and symbols through his sermons and discourses.

Though there are many differences among the four gospels in describing the life and ministry of Jesus, the gospels tell a remarkably similar story of Jesus' last days. While there are details in each gospel that are unique, the events of Jesus' Last Supper, arrest, trial, crucifixion, and death are quite parallel; probably because it was this event, and the resurrection that followed it, that started the Christian faith. Certainly it was the resurrection that moved the disciples of Jesus to begin to tell the stories and to proclaim Jesus as the Messiah and the hope of Israel. From that point, they began to baptize and draw people into a new relationship with God and one another.

Luke's gospel story, although similar to those in Mark and Matthew, does not end with the death and resurrection, but continues in a second "volume" called the Acts of the Apostles (sometimes referred to simply as "Acts"). This book tells the story of the apostles (those "sent" by Jesus, including the former disciples) as they begin their preaching and work. It centers on Peter and then moves to tell the story of Paul's conversion and mission to the Gentiles (those who are not Jewish). Again, this book may look like a "history" of the early church, but, like the gospels, its main purpose was not to relate verifiable historical information, but to demonstrate how the Christian faith spread from a few followers of Jesus to a movement that was found throughout the Roman Empire—even as far away as Rome itself.

While each gospel has an integrity of its own, it is clear that they are a compilation of many different recollections and stories from various Christian communities. It is thought that the earliest writings about Jesus were of two kinds. Accounts of his passion, death, and resurrection first circulated orally, as eyewitness accounts, and only later were written down. Next, collections of Jesus' sayings began to emerge from the early Christian communities from which the four gospels emerged. Some of these sayings were teachings about life and behavior, like the Sermon on the Mount recorded in Matthew 5 and Luke 4. Some of them were short, pithy sayings his followers remembered, like "some are last who will be first, and some are first who will be last" (Luke 13:30). Others are parables, like the parable of the sower (Mark 4:1–9), or sayings that have an apocalyptic theme, as they speak about the "end of all things" (see Mark 13). The gospel writers have taken these sayings and connected them to the story of Jesus' life, from his baptism until his arrest.

Though the gospels are the longest books in the New Testament, the most numerous writings in the Christians Scriptures are Paul's *letters* (sometimes called "epistles" after the Latin word for "letter"). These letters were written by Paul to several of the congregations he had founded. In addition to being the direct writings of one of the early preachers and expounders of the Christian message, they are also the earliest writings found in the New Testament, dating from between fifteen and thirty years after Jesus' death and resurrection. (By contrast, the gospels were written some decades later.) As such they are an important window into the formation and message of the earliest Christians. They were clearly held in great regard by the churches to which they were sent, because these communities saved them and apparently read from them on a regular basis in their worship and study.

These letters are, like most letters, addressed to specific situations and circumstances within the congregations to whom Paul is writing. Sometimes they seem a little opaque to those of us reading them some two thousand years later: since we only have Paul's side of the correspondence, we are not always sure just what Paul was writing about. He often refers to opponents, and seems to infer some of their teachings, but we do not always get a full picture of who they are. Still, we do get a clear picture of the basic message of Paul's ministry. We see how Paul began to apply his proclamation about Jesus not merely to "spiritual" things, but also to the way of life and the activities of his churches and their members. In this we perceive how Christianity quickly evolved from a simple message of salvation to a way of living day-to-day in the world.

The letters are typical of correspondence of the first century. Paul begins with a heading, telling us to whom he is writing and from whom the letter comes—in those days, the signature always came at the beginning rather than at the end of the letter. He then offers a greeting. Instead of "Dear So-and-So," he says, "Grace and peace to you. . . ." It is interesting to note that he does not offer these greetings from himself, but rather "from God the Father and the Lord Jesus Christ." Paul always saw himself as a representative of God, and in that role, he follows in the line of Hebrew prophets. The letters continue with advice, encouragement, and admonitions, and conclude with a blessing and, in some cases, personal greetings to individuals in the congregation. In addition to these letters of Paul, others are attributed to other Christian leaders in the early church, including Peter, James, and John. While tradition ascribes these letters to the early apostles, we also know it was common practice in the first century to attribute writings to well-known authority figures with circles of followers around them, so many scholars believe these letters were actually written by unnamed individuals within these communities who believed they were continuing the teachings of these apostles.

The Letter to the Hebrews, while traditionally called by that name, is actually a lengthy sermon on the topic of Jesus' superior priesthood. In fact, other "letters" in the New Testament may be of the same genre—not correspondence in our sense of the word, but a combination of preaching, teaching, and moral instruction for a particular church, or a group of churches. Ephesians, 1 and 2 Timothy, Titus, James, and 1 and 2 Peter are good examples.

The final book of the Christian Scriptures is the book of the Revelation to John. Like the Hebrew books of Daniel and Zechariah, Revelation is an *apocalyptic* work. It tells the story of a vision of heaven and of God's plans for the world in bringing the kingdom of God to its completion. Perhaps more than any other book in the Christian Scriptures, the apocalyptic book of Revelation has raised the difficult questions of interpretation to which we turn in the next chapter.

The Apocrypha

You may notice that in some versions of the Bible there are several books and some additions to other books of the Old Testament that are not usually found in Bibles used in Protestant churches. These additional writings may be interspersed within the Old and New Testaments or printed separately in a section called the *Apocrypha*—literally, "things that are hidden." Bibles with the books of the Apocrypha included tend to be used in Roman Catholic and Anglican churches, but less frequently in Protestant congregations, simply because the Protestant reformers of the fifteenth century used different sources for the ancient texts when translating their Bibles and did not hold these writings to be part of Scripture.

How did these books become part of some Bibles and not others? As we have seen, the Hebrew Scriptures developed over a long period of time, and the importance placed on specific books and texts also varied from generation to generation. In the first century BCE, a group of scholars in the Egyptian city of Alexandria undertook the task of translating the Hebrew Scriptures into Greek, so that Jews living outside Israel and speaking only Greek could hear and read the Bible in their own language. The Greek Septuagint was the Bible used by the early Christians, who mostly spoke Greek. It was also the Bible that Jerome translated into Latin (the Vulgate) as that language became the language of the church. Two centuries after the Septuagint, a group of Hebrew rabbis proposed an official version of the Hebrew Scriptures for Judaism—a canon that is still the basis for the *Tanakh*—which omitted several of the books included in the Septuagint. When the reformers of the church proposed a Bible, they took as the basis for their text these official Hebrew Scriptures and therefore omitted the Septuagint texts included in Roman Catholic versions.

Over the years Anglicans have held a mixed view on the texts of the Apocrypha, which have often been printed as a separate section within Bibles used in the Anglican churches, rather than intermingled with the books of the Old Testament, as in Roman Catholic Bibles. Some of these texts are among the Bible passages read aloud in churches during worship services, while others have not been included in the church's lectionary.

As with the Hebrew and Christian Scriptures, the books of the Apocrypha contain several different kinds of writings. Some are historical books, like 1 and 2 Maccabees, which tell the history of the Jewish revolt against foreign domination in the second century BCE, and various additions to the book of Ezra (1 Esdras). Some are stories, legends, or moralistic writings that read like novels, such as Tobit, Judith, Susanna, and Bel and the Dragon. The Apocrypha also includes books of teaching in the Wisdom tradition, namely the Wisdom of Solomon and Ecclesiasticus (sometimes called Sirach). Other books are devotional or liturgical in focus, like the Prayer of Manassah, the Prayer of Azariah, and the Song of the Three Young Men (sometimes called "additions to Daniel"). The prophetic writings of the Apocrypha include additions to Jeremiah and the book of Baruch, who was the prophet Jeremiah's secretary. Many of these writings contain apocalyptic elements, since they were written in the centuries after Israel's return from exile (400 to 100 BCE), during the times when the land was ruled by foreign governments and often overseen by hostile governors. Second Esdras is a primary example.

What value does the Apocrypha have? Clearly these texts have influenced the development and theological expression of the Christian faith. Several of the passages in 1 and 2 Esdras were important for the early church in interpreting the work of Jesus and his relationship to God. For example, in 2 Esdras we find a reference to "the Man," whom "the Most High has been keeping for many ages, who will himself deliver his creation; and he will direct those who are left" (13:26). Passages like these helped the early church interpret Jesus' title "Son of Man" as a description of the salvation that Jesus won.

From the books of the Apocrypha have also come many vivid literary works, as well as poetry and hymnody. Some proverbs and sayings from the Wisdom tradition are familiar to Anglicans because they are included in our lectionaries. This passage from the Wisdom of Solomon, for example, is often read at the Burial Office because it offers great comfort to the grieving and shares the Christian hope in the reality of God's life overcoming the power of death:

The souls of the righteous are in the hand of God,
and no torment will ever touch them.
In the eyes of the foolish they seemed to have died,
and their departure was thought to be a disaster,
and their going from us to be their destruction;
but they are at peace.
For though in the sight of others they were punished,
their hope is full of immortality. *(Wisdom 3:1–4)*

Like the rest of the Hebrew and Christian Scriptures, the books of the Apocrypha are both complex and straightforward, intriguing and baffling, soaring to great heights of the spirit and arousing heartfelt anger. Because they contain "things that are hidden," they raise for us profound questions of meaning and authority: Why are these books less scriptural than others? How exactly are we to know what the words of the Bible mean? And how are we to interpret its message for us today? We now turn to questions such as these.

Questions for Reflection and Discussion

1. How does knowing that the Bible was developed over a long period of time relate to the idea that it is the word of God? Does this make it harder or easier to think of the Bible as God's message to humankind?

2. Open a Bible to the table of contents, or the page that lists the books in the Old and New Testaments. Which books do you recognize from hearing them aloud in worship? What do you know about them? Which books are unfamiliar to you? In what section of the Bible are they found? Turn to a few of them, and see what you can discover about them.

3. Choose several passages from books in the Hebrew Scriptures and the Apocrypha and see if you can discern what type of literature you are reading. How might your interpretation of that passage be affected by knowing what type of literature it is?

4. Choose several passages from books in the Christian Scriptures and see if you can discern what type of literature you are reading. How might your interpretation of that passage be affected by knowing what type of literature it is?

How Do We Know
What the Bible Says?

The title for this chapter may seem a little odd. The Bible is a written document that has been translated into hundreds of different languages, so shouldn't it be obvious what the words on the pages mean? The difficulty for us in comprehending what the Bible says lies in the fact that the stories and sayings that eventually became the Bible were first handed down in oral form, and then written and copied by hand, edited, and interpreted for many thousands of years. Furthermore, the texts we read in English were originally spoken and written in languages very different from those we know today, and with every translation, decisions are made that affect the meaning of the texts, often in profound ways.[7]

We cannot know exactly what the "original" texts said since we do not have copies of those first writings and are so far removed from the time and culture when they were written, so of course there are difficulties in comprehending what is being said: that is the work of interpretation. Since we Christians call the Bible "the word of God," we want to be as clear and accurate as possible about what the Bible is saying, if we are to understand how God is addressing us and how we are invited to respond. This is not an easy task. How do we start to sort out what the Bible might be saying to us today?

THE FIRST INTERPRETERS

Across the centuries, within both the Jewish and Christian traditions, we find many different interpretations of the texts of the Hebrew and Christian Scriptures. Some books of the Bible seem to contradict other books, offering competing or varying descriptions of who God is, how God relates to humankind, and how we are to relate to God and to one another. For example, the two books of Samuel contain utterly different points of view on whether Israel should be allowed to have a king—both for and against. Contradictions occur with a single book as well—look at the two accounts of creation in Genesis 1 and 2. That is because the writers themselves began the process of interpreting the meaning of God's word long before these texts were collected into a single canon or book of Scripture. Within the different books of the Bible we find later passages that comment on, argue with, or reinterpret the meaning of earlier writings.

Sometimes these allusions are explicit, often beginning with "as it is written" and then going on to quote a particular passage word for word, recasting its meaning for a later generation. Jesus himself is practicing this sort of biblical reinterpretation of earlier texts when he discusses the well-known formula from Exodus 21, Leviticus 24, and Deuteronomy 19, laying out the measure of punishment to exact on wrongdoers:

> You have heard that it was said, "An eye for an eye and a tooth for a tooth." But I say to you, Do not resist an evildoer. But if anyone strikes you on the right cheek, turn the other also. (Matthew 5:38–39)

In most cases, the allusions to earlier books of the Bible take the form of borrowing an image, belief, or phrase and then reinterpreting or expanding upon its meaning. For example, later generations in Israel struggled with how to understand God as a "jealous God, punishing children for the iniquity of parents, to the third and the fourth generation" (Exodus 20:5). Evidently this belief in corporate punishment for the wrongs of an individual was being questioned by the time the book of Deuteronomy was being compiled, for its writers put forth a different law:

> Parents shall not be put to death for their children, nor shall children be put to death for their parents; only for their own crimes may persons be put to death. (Deuteronomy 24:16)

Again, Jesus is following in this Jewish tradition of interpretation when he takes the image of the prophet Jonah consigned to the belly of the sea monster for three days and three nights and sees it as foreshadowing his own death and descent to the depths of hell, "the heart of the earth." He goes on to use the story of Jonah to cast a stinging rebuke to the religious leaders who were questioning him:

> The people of Ninevah will rise up at the judgment with this generation and condemn it, because they repented at the proclamation of Jonah, and see, something greater than Jonah is here! (Matthew 12:41)

Like Jesus and countless rabbis and scholars before him, the authors of the later Hebrew Scriptures and the Christian Scriptures looked to the sacred books that would become the Bible and reinterpreted those books in their own writings—writings which would themselves later be included in the canon of the Scriptures. As one modern commentator observes, "Biblical authors bequeathed their successors not only a text, but ways of relating to that text, reacting to that text, recreating that text, and allowing that text to remain alive." Thus, he concludes, "the religion that *generated* the Bible foreshadows the religions *generated by* the Bible."[8]

Different Languages, Same Scriptures

When we are trying to understand the meaning of a particular passage of the Bible, we need to remember that the books of the Bible were written down over a long period of time, from about one thousand years before the common era until about two hundred years after the birth of Jesus. That is a span of over twelve hundred years! Think for a moment about the English language. If you have read early English texts (such as *Beowulf* or the writings of Chaucer), or even the more recent literature of Shakespeare from the sixteenth century, you know something has happened to the English language over those years. While we can recognize many of the words, the spellings and meanings have changed, and a great number of the words are completely unfamiliar—and it has only been about nine hundred years since *Beowulf* was written.

The biblical languages of Hebrew and Greek have undergone similar changes since the Bible was compiled, and this evolution was also taking place during the centuries the books of the Bible were being written and edited. In fact, the Hebrew and Greek in which the books of the Bible were written are not spoken any longer; modern Hebrew and Greek are markedly different languages. This means that when translators render the biblical Hebrew and Greek into modern English, they are not always certain of the original meanings of the words of the text. While most of the texts can be fairly well translated, there are portions that are obscure and uncertain. In those cases, translators must make judgments in order to develop a version of the text that is readable and coherent.

Even when dealing with the translation of modern languages, is often difficult to render a text into English. There may not be a word that exactly translates the original. For example, the English word "love" is used to translate four different Greek words that convey nuanced yet significant distinctions in meaning. Likewise, one of the most theologically important words in the Hebrew Scriptures can be translated into English as either "spirit" or "wind." Another can mean "word," "event," or "thing." This means a translator must decide what the original text meant; in other words, a translator must interpret the text.

This practice of translators debating the meaning of the text and how to render it into a contemporary language began in earnest a couple of centuries before the common era in Egypt, with the translation of the Hebrew Scriptures into Greek. After the over-throw of the kings in David's family in the sixth century BCE, many of the people of Israel and Judah left the Holy Land and moved to other cities and regions throughout the Mediterranean basin. There they began to speak the local languages, although Hebrew was apparently always used in their worship. Some of the Hebrew people in Egypt wanted to be able to hear the Scriptures read in the secular language they could understand, and so a group of rabbis and scholars translated much of the Hebrew Scriptures into the Greek, translation known as the Septuagint.

Since at this point in time there was not a definitive canon of Hebrew Scriptures, the Jewish scholars selected for translation the most widely known and used books. There are more books in the Septuagint than in the *Tanakh*, the official canon of the Hebrew Bible established in the second century CE (at least forty-six books in the Septuagint and only thirty-nine in the *Tanakh*). There are also differences in the order of some of the books (Psalms and Proverbs, for example), and some of the books are missing portions that are found in early Hebrew texts. These differences tell modern students of the Bible that the final texts of the Scriptures were not fixed in the ancient world, but may have varied from place to place and from version to version. It is one of the ways scholars have of trying to determine the oldest and most original versions of the stories and narratives of the Bible.

For Christians, the work of translating their Scriptures began with Jerome's fourth-century translation of the Hebrew Bible and many of the Christian writings of the New Testament into Latin, a translation that became known as the Vulgate (meaning the Bible in the vernacular, or common language of the people). Jerome was perhaps the greatest scholar of his day in the West, and was fluent in the three languages needed to translate the Bible at that time: Latin, Greek, and Hebrew. Most translators of the Bible into Latin before Jerome based their work on the Septuagint, since few knew Hebrew well enough to translate it accurately. Jewish scholars and rabbis had challenged some of the Christian interpretations of that Greek translation of the Hebrew Scriptures, however, and Jerome chose to go back to the original Hebrew sources because he recognized the validity of the rabbis' concerns. The Vulgate remained *the* Bible of the church in Europe throughout the Middle Ages, and its verses formed the basis for much of the liturgical texts of the Latin Mass.

As Latin increasingly became the language solely of scholars and clergy in the Middle Ages, the Vulgate ceased to be accessible for most people. Christians learned enough Latin to say a few prayers and memorize a few verses of Scripture, but as the Middle Ages drew to a close, for the most part the words of the Bible were unfamiliar, although there were a few translations of the Bible into other languages, such as Goth, Armenian, and Ethiopian. Translating the Bible into the language of the people was a cornerstone demand of the Protestant Reformation, and that concern for understanding the Scriptures has continued as translators through the ages have sought to make the Bible available to people in their own common language.

THE BIBLE IN ENGLISH

During the fifteenth and early sixteenth centuries, as the church's hold on learning and scholarship was being challenged, a new burst of translations of the Bible began. All across Europe, the Scriptures were being rendered from Latin into the language of the people. Martin Luther in Germany, John Calvin in Switzerland, and William Tyndale in England all brought the Bible into their native tongues. Tyndale's New Testament was published in 1526 and met with condemnation by the religious and governmental authorities because a Bible that could be read by people in the pew seemed to threaten official control over the interpretations of Scripture. Nevertheless, the work was popular and people were ready to hear and read the Bible in their own language. The invention of the printing press in the mid-fifteenth century allowed these new translations to become widely available. In England, this led to the production of many Bibles in modern languages, resulting finally in the production of the Authorized Version in 1611. This translation from the Greek and Hebrew texts was popularly called the King James Version because it was authorized by King James I of England.

And Protestants were not alone in desiring to have a Bible they could read in their own language. After the Reformation had taken hold, a Roman Catholic group also produced an English version of the Vulgate. It was not a new translation based on Greek and Hebrew sources, but a translation of the Latin Vulgate. It was known as the Douay-Rheims version and was produced at the beginning of the seventeenth century by scholars from the English Roman Catholic Church who had gone into exile in Holland after the coronation of Elizabeth I.

For many subsequent years there were only these two major English translations—the King James Version used by most Protestant churches, and the Douay-Rheims version used by Roman Catholic congregations. These two Bibles, each translated by committees of language scholars, represented the best scholarship of their time, as well as some of the best literature of their day. Until the middle of the twentieth century, these two versions were the only Bibles that most people heard in worship. In the Episcopal Church, for example, the King James Version was the only translation authorized for public reading in the church until the mid-twentieth century, and it is still beloved by many Christians throughout the world for its beautiful cadences and vocabulary. The same was true of the Douay-Rheims version in the Roman Catholic liturgies. There were other versions, mostly created by individual scholars, but they did not gain the acceptance of these two "official" translations.

In the 1940s and 1950s, the National Council of Churches of Christ, an ecumenical body of the major Protestant denominations, published a new version, the Revised Standard Version (RSV), which quickly became widely used. It was a new translation, based on new understandings about the original languages and customs of biblical times, but it also sought to maintain the literary traditions and formal language of the King James Version. In subsequent work, the RSV included the Apocrypha (or Deuterocanonical books) as well, and an ecumenical version of the RSV, known as the Common Bible, was given an imprimatur by the Roman Catholic Church.

If you look on the religion shelves of a large bookstore today, you will find many different versions of the Bible—perhaps a dozen or two. Some of the many English versions are reprints of the Bibles translated during and after the Reformation era, such as the King James Version, but many are modern translations, like the New Revised Standard Version or the New Revised English Bible. In our time there has been a flurry of interest in translating the Bible. Modern study of the Bible has resulted in a much better understanding of the texts and languages of the Scriptures, and this means that scholars can render a more accurate reading of the text. But scholarship has also created controversy, which has resulted in conflict between various theological factions and groups within the Christian tradition. So a number of the modern versions of the Bible have been translated with doctrinal and confessional interests as a factor in the translators' work. This can be seen in the difference in translation of Luke 1:42b between the New Revised Standard Version (an ecumenical translation) and the New Jerusalem Bible (a Roman Catholic translation). The NRSV reads: "Blessed are you among women. . . ," while the New Jerusalem's translation supports the Roman Catholic doctrine of Mary's special status: "Of all women you are the most blessed. . . ."

When you are looking for a Bible to use for personal reading and study, it is important to understand the approach taken by the translators. In the resource section at the end of this book we provide a brief overview of some of the more popular modern versions you may encounter.

Clearly there are more English versions of the Bible available today than any one person would need to use. For Bible study it is good to have several translations at hand in order to compare the renderings of certain passages, and to see if there are any words or ideas that seem difficult to translate into English. Comparing passages can often lead to a fuller understanding of what the text is trying to say. If you prefer the "readability" of a translation that uses more paraphrase, it is still good to keep a word-for-word translation handy to check against more interpreted versions.

DIFFERENT CULTURES, DIFFERENT INTERPRETATIONS

The translation of the words of the Bible from one language to another is one important way the meaning of those words has been interpreted through the centuries. Translators study not only the languages themselves, but also their modern versions and other related languages to try to determine the likely meaning of words that may be obscure or whose definition or usage may have changed over time. As they also examine non-biblical documents from a particular era, they can often determine the meaning of words by examining their use in other contexts.

Yet the task of interpreting the Bible has not stopped with questions about the meanings of particular words—although in a document called the word of God, the words would seem pretty important! Scholars also look for the most ancient versions of the text, since we do not have any of the original writings of the books of the Bible. We do have a few fragmentary ancient texts, but most of our complete books of the Bible come from the Middle Ages, when texts were dictated and copied by monks to make them widely available to churches and schools. This process inevitably introduced errors and changes in the text: no matter how careful they might be, the monks might misread or incorrectly hear the text being read aloud as they wrote, or texts may have been altered copies themselves. In addition, as with the Hebrew Scriptures, over time comments or interpretations (called *glosses*) scribbled in the margins by these copyists were incorporated into the text itself. Unfortunately the monks also had the thrifty but historically tragic habit of recycling the old copy when they finished a new one, drastically reducing the number of older versions available to us today. So contemporary scholars gather the texts they have, compare them and study their agreements and differences, and seek to determine which variants are most likely the closest to the original words and meanings. This sort of biblical interpretation is termed *textual criticism*.

There is also a long and rich history of Jewish rabbis and doctors of Jewish law who, both orally and in written texts, have interpreted and reinterpreted the terms of the law and the meaning of their Scriptures. The work of rabbis in the first five centuries of the common era is specifically called *midrash*, meaning "to inquire" or "to search after," and is compiled in a text called *Midrash Rabbah*. Other rabbinic interpretations include anthologies called the *Mishna* and the *Gemara* (together called the *Talmud*), which are as much revered in Judaism as the Hebrew Scriptures themselves, though the Torah is always the primary authority.

These early rabbinic and Christian scholars laid important foundations for interpretation that later theologians would draw upon in their own study of the Scriptures. They viewed the Bible as a single document, and thus attempted to make connections among all the various books. Sometimes this meant taking phrases or verses out of context or making interpretive connections among verses that originally had none—practices that Christians adopted quite freely. Some Jewish commentators, inspired by the Greek tradition of allegorizing their myths, developed *allegorical* interpretations of the biblical stories. These "spiritual" meanings for the literal texts might be quite simple, or they could become so far removed from the literal meaning as to seem bizarre or far-fetched to the modern mind, which places a higher value on a literal sense of the text.

As the church grew and evolved, Christian teachers and scholars took up the same work of interpretation as the Jewish rabbis. We have writings from early church leaders and teachers, often called the "church fathers," that go back as far as the second century of the common era, and many of them contain allegorical interpretations of Paul's writings as well as of Jesus' ministry, life, and death. Most of these commentators began by looking for a hidden, often moral meaning underneath the literal text of the Bible. By using allegory as a device to unearth the deeper meaning, these early Christian biblical interpreters developed a way of instructing people in the faith and discerning the theological depths of the biblical story.

An example of this kind of allegorical interpretation can be found in Mark's account of the parable of the sower. Jesus tells the story of the sower scattering seeds on different kinds of earth; some seeds wither and die, while others flourish in good soil, "increasing and yielding thirty and sixty and a hundredfold" (Mark 4:2–9). Mark then offers an allegory: the story is about the different ways God's word of salvation is received. Some welcome the gospel gladly but renounce it in the face of persecution; others are choked by "the cares of the world, and the lure of wealth"; only the faithful "hear the word and accept it and bear fruit" (Mark 4:13–20).

Thus the allegory often changes the story's meaning by detecting a "moral" that the story may not have intended to convey.

Such methods of interpretation were used not only to explain and deepen the faith of Christians, but also to defend that faith to those outside the church by using methods similar to those of secular scholars. This theological method is called an *apology*, the Greek word for "defense," designed to show that Christianity is a reasonable and useful approach to living. Early Christian fathers also defended the faith by using a common interpretive technique known as *typology*. These teachers looked at many of the texts of the Hebrew Scripture as "types" or foreshadowings of the events and characters in the Christian Scriptures. For example, the story of the sacrifice of Isaac was seen as prefiguring the story of Jesus' sacrifice: the early Christian image of Jesus as the lamb who was slain. Similarly, the "scapegoat" described in Leviticus, slain for the collective guilt of the community, was a "type" that helped explain the purpose and meaning of Jesus' death as atoning for the sins of the world. Paul uses the story of the creation of Adam in Genesis to point to Christ as the "second Adam" (1 Corinthians 15:22; Romans 5:12). These reinterpretations of the Hebrew Scriptures helped Christians find meaning in those texts that strengthened and inspired their understandings of Jesus, and were used to refute the claims of some in the early church that the Hebrew Scriptures were no longer valid.

Some of this interpretive study was a result of the growth of the Christian movement in the Greek and Roman cultures. Although the earliest followers of Jesus were Jewish, the widespread incorporation of Gentile believers into the church and the spread of Christian congregations into Asia and Greece forced Christians to recast their beliefs in different cultures and languages, just as the Jewish people had done during times of exile. New ways of thinking about Jesus and his life, death, and resurrection began to emerge. The apostle Paul was among the first to engage in this kind of evangelism, and in Paul's writings we can see the beginnings of the influence of Greek thought on his preaching of the gospel to the different cultures in which he found himself.

THE DEVELOPMENT OF CHRISTIAN INTERPRETATION

Doctrinal questions about the nature of God and Jesus dominated much of the early church's theology. In the fourth and fifth centuries the theological interpretation of the Scriptures became an important part of the formation of the creeds and other foundational statements of the church's faith. During this time, the study of Scripture on such issues as Christology—the nature of Jesus Christ (was he God, man, or both?)—was predominant. This *theological* interpretation of the Bible generated a great deal of controversy, but ultimately a broad consensus of beliefs about Jesus and the nature of biblical interpretation emerged. With these methods theologians searched the Bible for support of the doctrines and developments of Christian theology. While these methods were important, Augustine of Hippo summed up the ultimate measure of their value when he said: "Whoever thinks that he understands the Holy Scriptures, or any part of them, but puts such an interpretation upon them as does not tend to build up this twofold love of God and our neighbour, does not yet understand them."[9]

During the Middle Ages, especially with the eleventh-century renaissance in scholarly biblical learning, a wealth of Jewish and Christian reinterpretations of the Scriptures emerged and laid some of the foundations for the later Reformation of the church. The Jewish scholar known as Rashi, for example, emphasized the "contextual meaning of Scripture": he opposed the earlier practice of freely taking verses out of context and constructing detailed meanings from a single isolated verse. Martin Luther would later incorporate many of the interpretations of Rashi into his own commentaries on the books of the Hebrew Scriptures.

The preeminent thirteenth-century Christian scholar Thomas Aquinas also viewed the literal sense of the words of the Bible as the most important: "All the senses are founded on one, the literal, from which alone any argument can be drawn, and not from those intended in allegory."[10] The elaborate allegorical interpretations so popular with church fathers like Origen were valuable in shedding light on the spiritual meaning of Scripture, he believed, but they must first be based on the literal meaning of the text. In addition to this literal meaning, medieval theologians used a number of other methods of interpretation in their study of the Bible, going beyond the allegorical to include the moral and eschatological (or anagogical). Their purposes can be summed up in the Latin verse that was popular at the time:

> The letter shows us what God and our fathers did;
> The allegorical shows us where our faith is hid;
> The moral meaning gives us rules of daily life;
> The anagogy shows us where we end our strife.[11]

In other words, the literal meaning conveyed the historical or actual story told in a passage, while the allegorical revealed its spiritual dimension. The moral sense helped to develop guidelines for the conduct of daily human life, and the eschatological interpretation revealed the ultimate hope for the end of time. In passages about the city of Jerusalem, to cite a common example, medieval theologians might see a geographical place, a "heavenly Jerusalem" that is the home of all who believe in God, a Jerusalem that provides a place for learning moral conduct within a just society, and the land of "milk and honey" that is our ultimate destiny and hope.

As the Middle Ages came to an end, new questions and debates about the meaning of Scripture began to emerge. In the Renaissance biblical scholars came to view the recovery of the Scriptures in their original languages of Hebrew and Greek as mandatory. The invention of the printing press in the mid-fifteenth century, which made possible the publication of the Bible for a wider audience, fueled the urge to "return to the sources." In late-fifteenth-century Spain, the first Greek New Testament to appear as part of a set that included the Latin Vulgate and the Hebrew Scriptures in Hebrew and in Greek was published. The printing press also required a more uniform version of the biblical texts than was required during the age of hand-copying, so editors had to make decisions about which of the various manuscripts circulating at the time were *the* authoritative texts to print—decisions that would establish the standard texts for centuries to come.

The availability of the Scriptures in their original languages and in a variety of vernacular languages as well led to the Reformation of the church in the sixteenth century, as different interpretations of those Scriptures emerged. People like Martin Luther and John Calvin began to read the Bible outside the usual framework provided by the church, and that reading led them to challenge official doctrine in ways that eventually caused them to leave the church of Rome. Their interpretive framework eliminated the ancient tools of doctrine, typology, and allegory, and instead relied on the internal connections and references within the Bible to provide the meaning and interpretation. Their cry was *sola Scriptura*: "by Scripture alone." Even this foundational stance was subject to varying interpretations among Protestants, however: for Calvin, for example, only those church practices explicitly commanded in the Bible were allowed, while for Luther practices were allowed unless explicitly forbidden. These two basic principles can still be seen at work in many Protestant churches today.

The methods of the reformers undermined the hierarchical, "top-down" practice of interpretation and instead placed much interpretive power in the hands of individual believers. This major shift in authority led to a proliferation of interpretations and to an upsurge in the number of denominations and church sects, such as the various churches following the interpretations of Luther and Calvin, and the heirs of the Anabaptist tradition. As Jaroslav Pelikan has commented, "The rule of the sole authority of Scripture meant in practice the unquestioned authority of this or that particular interpretation of Scripture as it was characteristic of this or that church body."[12] To shore up their own interpretation and at the same time uphold the authority of the Bible as the source of their authority, reformers also found it necessary to define more closely *how* the books of the Bible were of divine inspiration. Their debates led some to the conclusion that the Bible must be without error— "inerrant"—in every word and detail, from the age of the world and the geographical location of the Garden of Eden to the stories of angels and wise men visiting the infant Jesus in Bethlehem.

Although printed versions of the Latin Vulgate and several vernacular translations existed long before the Reformation, the reformers particularly valued the original languages of Scripture and worked to translate the Bible from Hebrew and Greek into the languages of their communities. Martin Luther's German Bible became the standard for all German translations; John Calvin in French-speaking Switzerland and William Tyndale and Miles Coverdale in England likewise produced outstanding translations.

The availability of printed Bibles that people could actually read for themselves, coupled with increasing literacy among the laity and an emphasis in both Protestant and Catholic churches on an educated clergy, brought about a revival in spirituality and popular piety in the church. While in the Middle Ages people learned the stories of the Bible through preaching and the portrayal of those stories in stained-glass windows, after the sixteenth century the Bible became the central focus of their piety in ways it had never been before. The laity began to expect and demand more detailed exposition of biblical passages in the sermons they heard in worship, as they undertook studies of the Bible in church groups. This shift toward a Bible-based Christian spirituality spread across Protestant and Catholic lines. In the Catholic Reformation the Roman Church attempted to incorporate the rediscovered authority of Scripture into its liturgical, preaching, spiritual, and educational life, though it continued to uphold the place of the church's tradition in its interpretation of biblical texts in ways the more radical Protestant churches did not.

NEW TIMES, NEW INTERPRETATIONS

The Reformation era was a time of explosive expansion in biblical scholarship. Scholarly journals began to appear, and, supported by the rise of modern universities, conversations among biblical scholars within the Jewish, Roman Catholic, and Protestant traditions took place as never before. As the decades of religious fervor and violent conflict wore themselves out and the Enlightenment unfolded, scholars from all three traditions continued and expanded their work on the historical-critical study of the books of the Bible.

One of the fundamental tensions beneath their work was the question of the authority and truth of the Bible. The Reformation view of the Bible as divinely inspired and thus authoritative was difficult to reconcile with the apparent contradictions and errors of historical or scientific fact within the Scriptures themselves. Likewise, how were believers to know which version of the ancient text was the "true" one? The Enlightenment's solution was to apply the same historical-critical methods of study and interpretation to the sacred texts of the Bible as were being applied to other ancient writings. These scholars asked troubling questions like, Who actually wrote the books of the Bible? Traditionally Moses was the author of the first five books of the Bible, for example, but if Moses was the author, how did he write the chapter at the end of Deuteronomy describing his own death? And if Moses did not in fact write those books, why did Jesus ascribe them to him? Was he simply following in the tradition of his time so as not to upset his hearers, or did he in fact share in their belief the texts were written by Moses? If so, how could the Son of God be mistaken? Furthermore, the discoveries of geology and the natural sciences, plus the theories of Darwin, troubled many Anglican clergy and presented a serious challenge to biblical scholars of the nineteenth century.

Scholars therefore attempted to reconcile the findings of this historical-critical method with their belief in the truth and divine authority of the texts they studied, but with varying degrees of success. These troubling contradictions weighed most heavily on those Protestants who could not accept the explanation of certain passages in allegorical or spiritual terms, or the possibility of errors in the transmission or translation of the Bible. This wholesale rejection of critical study of the Bible and an insistence that every word of the text is literally true continues as a powerful force within certain churches.

Today the study of the Bible incorporates an even wider variety of perspectives than in previous generations. Modern biblical criticism has a number of disciplines, all growing out of the Enlightenment urge to apply human reason to the world and all of its expressions. Some scholars are working from a faith perspective, seeking to demonstrate the truth of the Bible and its narratives, while others reject faith in such things as miracles and resurrections from the dead and instead focus on the central moral teachings of

Scripture. Some wish to engage in a conversation between religion and reason, applying contemporary intellectual understandings and criteria to the biblical text, while others use the theories of Marx and the social scientists. With so many approaches to biblical study and interpretation available to us, we are given a rich—if sometimes confusing—array to choose from when we approach Bible study today.

THE VALUE OF BIBLICAL CRITICISM

What are some of these methods, and why are they important to our understanding of the Bible? Every time we use a study Bible or open a commentary, we are exposed to the insights of the *historical-critical* method. Scholars using this method try to discover the historical circumstances out of which the various books arose, using the disciplines of archaeology and the dating of ancient texts. For some of these scholars, verifying the Bible's version of events and hence its historical reliability is a prime concern.

Sometimes this method yields quite interesting results. For example, key stories in Genesis are related to the myths of other cultures of the same era: both the story of creation and the story of Noah and the great flood are reflected in similar stories in Babylonian and Canaanite writings. Likewise, other cultures have annals of their kings similar to those found in the Hebrew books of Kings and Chronicles, and comparing these texts with those of the Hebrew Scriptures deepens our understanding of both. The Israelites were clearly much influenced by the cultures around them, though it is also clear that the biblical stories have a very different perspective about God. New Testament studies of the Jewish groups that were in conversation and conflict with Jesus (such as the Pharisees and Sadducees) have helped us understand more accurately the nature of the differences between Jesus and his followers and other faithful Jewish sects and parties of that time.

The growth in archaeological discoveries has also been an important part of historical-critical study. Through the discovery of ancient texts, cities, and buildings, scholars have been able to understand more fully the cultures, customs, narratives, beliefs, and events recorded in the Bible. For instance, the "quest for the historical Jesus" has been a particular focus of the past twenty years. Many scholars have tried to see Jesus in terms of the culture and milieu of his time, trying to temper the gospel writers' Christian view of Jesus with a more "objective" vision. While it has raised a number of interesting ideas and fundamentally changed the way many Christians understand Jesus, this quest still seems somewhat elusive, and many scholars believe it is simply not possible to see Jesus apart from the gospel lens through which he was viewed at the time.

If historical criticism examines and tests the reliability of biblical accounts, *literary criticism* asks, "What can this text tell us about the different kinds of literature that make up the Bible?" This method analyzes the text for literary forms—hymns, letters, poems, genealogy, narrative—and for signs of editing and alteration. Scholars have discovered that within the written texts we have available, a variety of sources have been at work. For example, in Genesis, it appears that the final editors used four different sources to tell the story of our beginnings, each with its own style, vocabulary, and even theology. Likewise, it appears that in the New Testament the authors of Luke and Matthew drew directly from the gospel of Mark as their primary source. This concern for knowing where the text has come from, and how it was edited into its final form has led to a school of *source criticism*, which looks at both internal and external material to try to determine how the text of the Bible came to be and from what original sources.

Form criticism tries to discover the "original life situation" of different kinds of biblical literature. It has been helpful in understanding the Psalms in their original liturgical setting, for example, and, in the New Testament, it sheds new light on the "conflict stories" between Jesus and his adversaries.

Other contemporary scholars look at the whole of Scripture, rather than fragmenting it into texts or categories. Writers from the humanities, such as Northrop Frye and Robert Alter, have helped us read the biblical story as great literature made up of powerful and enduring characters and themes. Brevard Childs and his students have also looked at the Bible as we have it in its present form and helped us see the theological perspectives behind the various parts of the Bible. As *canonical* critics, these scholars want to ask, "How does the text of the Bible speak to us as a whole, rather than as a sum of its various parts?"

Christians can use some or all of these scholarly approaches to Scripture to deepen their understanding of what the Bible says to us today. They can examine the results of biblical scholarship through the lens of their faith, and see how it gives new light to the word of God in the Bible. For example, in recognizing there are two different stories of the creation in the book of Genesis, some have concluded that the creation story is not a scientific description of *how* God created the universe, but rather a profound explanation of *why* God created it. This synthesis allows these Christians to find a place for modern scientific approaches to creation and evolution while upholding their belief in the truth and relevance of the Bible.

One of the side effects of this scholarly study of the Bible is that many people feel the Bible is too complicated to be understood without a rigorous knowledge of the various methods of interpretation, so they put the Bible aside as incomprehensible and irrelevant to their lives. It is thus important for us to remember that what scholars look for in the Bible (and in any literature they study) is not what most Christians look for in their Holy Book. The story of Jesus in the gospels, his ministry and teachings, his death and resurrection; the stories of the people of Israel, with their wanderings, errors, defeats, and renewals; the words of the prophets; Paul's letters and the history of the early church's experience: all are accessible and easily read—and, for the most part, can be understood without a library of interpretive aids. For centuries religious people have done just that, as they heard or read the stories of Scripture, reflected on and interpreted them, and discerned the application of the Bible's message to their own lives and situations. We too can grasp a basic notion of what the Bible is saying, regardless of our level of scholarship; we can listen to a passage read in a church service and gain an understanding of its meaning.

That said, even a cursory grasp of modern and traditional biblical scholarship *does* help to deepen our understanding of how the Bible was formed and the meaning of its texts. These aids undoubtedly help us to understand more accurately and fully the message of the Bible and to avoid pitfalls of interpretation that can distort the meaning of the texts, and can thus stifle or undermine our faith. The Bible may be beloved by many, but it is also widely rejected because of misunderstandings of its meaning and message. Gaining a deeper understanding of what the Bible is saying takes time and effort, but such effort can be life-changing as the words of the Bible become full of significance and reveal the God we yearn to know and trust. The task and responsibility of each Christian to delve into a study of the Bible has, at least since the Reformation, been an important dimension of discipleship. It is perhaps even more essential today, as Christians argue over how to interpret and apply the words of Scripture to the world in which we live.

QUESTIONS FOR REFLECTION AND DISCUSSION

1. Gather several translations of the Bible, including one or two study Bibles. Choose a passage from the Psalms and compare them. Which words are different? How do they change the meaning of the passage? Can you discern why the translators might have chosen to render the passage in that way? What do you think might be the historical context for the text? How could you find out? What difference would it make?

2. Now choose passages from one of the gospels and from one of the New Testament letters, and ask similar questions of those texts.

3. What do you think about how the Bible is used by various Christian traditions to interpret the political and social issues of our day?

4. How do you think we are able to trust the Bible to be an accurate rendition of what God wants human beings to know?

The Bible in the Church's Life

A recent radio news story told of the efforts of perhaps two hundred Indian Jews who were born and raised in India to migrate to Israel so they might live in the land of their religious ancestors. A group of American Christians was sending the financial resources necessary to make the journey, and the basis for their generosity, according to the reporter, was a promise in the book of Genesis that God would bless those who blessed the children of Israel. What are we to make of this story? Were these Christians being foolishly naïve, taking a verse from an ancient document completely out of context and applying it literally to their own checkbooks? Or were they being incredibly faithful, responding to God's timeless and ongoing call to care for his chosen people? Who is to say? How do we know?

This story, and many like it, illustrate a powerful and pervasive question we in the church continually face: *What is the authority of the Bible in the church's life?* How much influence do the words of the Bible have to determine the way we live, the moral stands we take, the choices we make? Most Christian churches recognize that the Bible has authority over the teaching and doctrines they profess; that is, their teachings and doctrines are not to contradict the Bible. Yet the stance we take toward the authority of the Bible is not merely an interesting point of conversation within the church; it has far-reaching ramifications for almost every aspect of how we live out our faith in a complex and multicultural world. Many individual Christians also accept the Bible's authority over their personal lives, seeing in the ethical and legal instructions of the Bible a guide for their personal behavior. We look to the Bible for direction regarding the values we should hold and the ethical behaviors we should practice, and that direction is not always easy to discern clearly, for several reasons.

First, the texts of the Bible are broad and diverse enough to encompass widely divergent views, and verses are often taken out of context in order for people on opposing sides of every issue to quote passages to support their positions. If the Bible were merely a book with a single vision setting forth timeless truths beyond the reach of culture and historical circumstance, applying those teachings to our daily lives and institutions might be fairly straightforward. But as we have seen, the books of the Bible were written by people who lived in specific times and places, and while the Bible can be consistently clear about some matters of law and doctrine, it can also give mixed messages. For example, both the Hebrew and Christian Scriptures are in agreement about upholding the laws known as the Ten Commandments: God's people must not worship idols, must not commit murder, should honor their parents, and so on—yet Christians keep Sunday as their day of worship, and do not see an obligation to rest on the Sabbath. Likewise, in the Hebrew Scriptures it is an absolute requirement for males to be circumcised in order to be part of the faithful Jewish community, yet in the Christian Scriptures this requirement is set aside for Gentiles who wished to be baptized into the church.

Furthermore, it is easy to affirm the authority of the Bible when its message is congruent with the humane values of our society at its best—"life, liberty, and the pursuit of happiness." But if we accept that the Bible is authoritative in our lives, what do we do with passages that seem to contradict values we hold dear? In a world that knows genocide and horrific crimes against the innocent, how can we embrace those texts in the Hebrew Scriptures that seem to encourage the annihilation of entire tribes of people? How should we understand the New Testament's apparent acceptance of slavery and sanctioning of cultural norms in which women were to remain silent in church and submissive to men?

Even when we acknowledge the authority of the Bible to influence the way we live, applying the words of the Bible to our lives is not a simple matter. There are as many interpretations of the Bible as there are interpreters. Can any and all interpretations be true? Are there tools we can use to help us understand how the message of the Bible is supposed to affect our daily lives: the jobs we hold, the people for whom we vote, the way we raise our children, the values we live by, the institutions we create to express and support our religious beliefs? News stories are filled with terrible examples of people who interpret the words of Scripture as mandates for violence or control or judgment of others, as well as stories in which the words of the Bible motivated people to brave self-sacrifice or untold generosity. So how do we as a church community discern which interpretations of the Bible are a true revelation of God and of what God asks human beings to do? How do we know which viewpoints are truly good news and which are words of false judgment or fantasy?

Finally, how do we decide which interpretations are urgently relevant for those of us in the church *today*? Many of the laws and regulations of the Bible are bound to the particular times and cultures in which they were developed and must be interpreted and adapted to our time and situation. How do we know which teachings demand obedience and which are no longer applicable to us? For the Jews and Gentiles of Paul's day, for example, the question of whether Christians were obliged to keep Jewish dietary laws was pressing and therefore the subject of many sermons, letters, and teachings—some of which have found their way into our New Testament. For most of us in the church today, that question has largely receded into the realm of history. We have our own urgent concerns, from abortion to global warming to the ordination of homosexual persons, and the Bible does not give definitive answers to these questions. Yet the biblical stories describing the *process* of how the early church resolved their topics of controversy and the methods they used to discover what they should do, how they should live, what religious practices they should embrace—those remain valuable interpretive tools for us as we deal with the pressing concerns of our own day.

In *Biblical Authority or Biblical Tyranny?* New Testament scholar L. William Countryman clearly identifies the confusion we face:

> The same chapter that tells us not to work on Saturday also tells us not to commit murder. How does one know that the one commandment still avails and the other does not? The very same verse (Lev. 19:26) that forbids witchcraft also forbids eating meat that has not been slaughtered in a kosher way. How does the Christian "know" that the one commandment still holds and the other does not?[13]

Countryman goes on to explain that the authority of God cannot reside in any single book, though we may wish that it could. We wish we could simply read the Bible and know God's will for us. But the Bible is not God. Rather, it is a book that is "the work of human minds and lips and hands, under the inspiration of God."

This notion of the Bible as "inspired" is one key to understanding the authority of the Bible in our lives. Many people confuse the concept of inspiration—which means "filling with Spirit"—with a belief in the inerrancy of the biblical texts. We have a hard time shaking the simplistic yet powerful image of God "dictating" the words of the Bible to people who wrote them down verbatim. And yet inspiration and inerrancy are two completely separate notions. Christians can in fact embrace the Bible as the inspired word of God and at the same time not hold that all its words are without factual error or applicable for all times and places. When we believe the Bible to be inspired by God, we are saying its texts are filled with God's Spirit and their truths in some way therefore transcend the time and place and human limitations through which the words were written. We come to know the God of the Bible through our study and interpretation of the words of the Bible, but we must always remember that God is not limited to nor definitively described for all time by the biblical writers, who knew and experienced God in a particular place and time, just as we do.

At the same time, while the infinite God cannot be contained within the limited words of the Bible, we are finite creatures living in a particular place at a specific time in history. We can only know

God through earthly means—like words and stories, bread and wine, ourselves and other people. So it is the Christian communities around the world, Countryman believes, that must be the "practical authorities" for interpreting the Bible. The ways these Christian communities embody that authority will vary, of course: some churches are more comfortable with a hierarchical structure with only a few bishops holding the authority to interpret Scripture; others will choose a more democratic structure of scholars and teachers taking the lead in interpretation, or will place the authority within a written document such as a creed or doctrinal statement. Whatever the means through which a particular community exercises its authority, the Bible always remains in a sense outside it, reminding us that we do not know everything there is to know about God. As Countryman notes, "The Bible, then, is the principal condition of life and growth for the faithful, for it forbids us to suppose that our present is the sum total of human life under God."[14]

AUTHORITY AND CONTROVERSY

This issue of biblical authority is at the center of nearly all of the controversies over which the church has argued throughout its history, from slavery and homosexuality to the nature of Christ and the sinlessness of Mary, from just war theories and the divine right of monarchs to how to address world poverty and the role of women in the church. Article XX of the *Articles of Religion*, a sixteenth-century statement by the Church of England regarding a variety of church teachings, says this about authority:

> The Church hath power to decree Rites or Ceremonies, and authority in Controversies of Faith: and yet it is not lawful for the Church to ordain any thing that is contrary to God's Word written, neither may it so expound one place of Scripture, that it be repugnant to another. (BCP 871)

The article goes on to say that while the church is a keeper of the Bible, it is not to decree anything that is in opposition to it, nor to teach as a means for obtaining salvation anything that is not from it. In other words, the church has the power to reinterpret the traditions it has received in light of the new challenges it faces in each generation, but those new interpretations may not contradict the teaching of Scripture. Coming to some general agreement on what "the teaching of Scripture" is exactly on a particular issue or concern, however, is often problematic.

For example, when the Episcopal Church began to consider ordaining women as bishops and priests, many people raised serious questions about the leadership of women based on the passages in the New Testament that were opposed to women taking a leading role in the churches. During the discussions the passages that were explicitly opposed to women assuming positions of leadership (1 Corinthians 14:34, for example, which states that "women should be silent in the churches") were weighed against other passages that indicated women were actually assuming leadership roles as apostles, benefactors, and fellow workers (see Romans 16:3–6 and Matthew 28, for example). The church also considered passages suggesting that Christ brought about a new social order of equality among men and women in which "there is no longer male and female" (Galatians 3:27–29).

Two important principles are at work in this example. First, the church cannot alter the long-standing teachings of the Christian faith without prayerfully and thoughtfully asking, "What does Holy Scripture tell us about these things?" Second, specific passages in the Bible that seem to be prohibitive may be counterbalanced by looking at other passages and asking, "What is the larger message of the Bible about these things?" In this way, we can see the church taking Scripture's authority seriously, without setting aside the real challenges and concerns for relevance brought about by changes in the cultural and social conditions of our time.

While the church might tell us that the Bible has explicit and final authority, we can see that the Bible's authoritative word is often tempered and reinterpreted by theological and practical concerns that have arisen during the last two thousand years. We all use the Bible both to support the beliefs we want to hold and to refute those beliefs we reject. Since the Bible is rarely allowed to speak its message unencumbered by the hopes and needs of its read-

ers or preachers or teachers, we are continually obliged to be aware
of the personal and cultural filters through which we proclaim and
receive that message. How does the church in every age arrive at
these decisions as to what is congruent with the teaching of
Scripture and what is not?

Over the centuries the church has developed strategies for identifying and evaluating the filters that shape our interpretation of the
gospel message. In the Episcopal Church, tradition, reason, and
Scripture—often called the "three-legged stool" in Anglican teaching—have been essential tools. While the Bible is our primary
source for understanding God and God's relationship to humanity,
for Episcopalians these two other sources of revelation must always
come into play. Just as when any one of the three legs of a stool
is removed or shortened the stool will fall, so when the church
neglects to give due consideration to Scripture, tradition, and
reason equally, the foundation of our common life is distorted or
becomes lopsided.

TRADITION AS AN INTERPRETER OF SCRIPTURE

One leg of the stool, tradition, includes the ways the church
throughout history has understood and interpreted the revelation
of God in the Bible. For Anglicans, tradition is more a spectrum of
interpretations outlining the boundaries of acceptable Christian
beliefs than a fixed statement of a single perspective.

The creeds are one example of the church's tradition. The
Apostles' Creed is based on an early baptismal formula; the
Athanasian and Nicene Creeds were developed later by councils of
the church gathered to discuss and discern the limits of orthodox
("right belief") descriptions of God. The creeds are a kind of
summary of what Scripture tells us about God, as the church has
interpreted that witness through its experience of God. In that sense
the creeds explain and extend the witness of Scripture, and give us
a model for how our experience can reinterpret and shed light on
the revelation of God in the Bible.

For example, most of the first Christians believed in the God of
the Hebrew Scriptures. Through their experience of Jesus they also
came to believe that God had become uniquely incarnate in this

particular man and had lived among them. After the death and resurrection of Jesus these earliest disciples began to describe him not only as the Son of Man but as the Son of God. And as they experienced the Son of God present among them when gathered for prayer and worship and "the breaking of the bread," Christians began to describe their sense of spiritual awakening to God's presence within them in terms of God's Spirit or the Holy Spirit. Thus because of this experience the early church began to use language for God that would become the Holy Trinity described in the creeds: God the Father, Son, and Holy Spirit, or God the Creator, Redeemer, and Sanctifier.

While the earliest writings in the New Testament do not explicitly use trinitarian language to talk about God, by the time Matthew's gospel appeared, the church was baptizing converts "in the name of the Father and of the Son and of the Holy Spirit" (Matthew 28:19). The story of the Holy Spirit descending on the day of Pentecost as a "violent wind" and tongues of fire likewise led the earliest Christians to speak of God as Father, Son, and Holy Spirit. Theologians in the first few centuries after Jesus reasoned that this way of describing God as a Trinity of persons fit with the teachings of Scripture, and made sense both in light of the church's experience and as philosophical terms understood by Christians who were Greeks rather than Hebrews. This "tradition" of interpretation and elaboration of the scriptural understandings of God took place over several centuries, and provided the background to the formal creedal expressions that emerged from the fourth- and fifth-century councils of Nicaea and Chalcedon. Subsequent theological conversation and writing has continued to affirm these traditional statements.

In the Anglican Church, the creeds have been an important part of our understanding of the Christian faith. In the late nineteenth century, Anglicans formally set up a standard for the key elements of Christian teaching. This Anglican "Quadrilateral" states that a full expression of the Christian faith will include four elements: Scripture, the creeds, the two biblical sacraments (baptism and Eucharist), and the historic apostolic ministry. This means that for Episcopalians, the Bible, sacraments, ministry, and creeds are the primary traditions that the church has passed down through the centuries.

In a sense, then, tradition is the ongoing revelation of God in every culture through the years. It expresses the ways Christians in a certain time and place understood and interpreted their experience of God after the closing of the canon of Scripture. Tradition can be somewhat time-bound, and the church is continually reevaluating the traditions it receives. At the time of the Reformation, for example, many Christians decided that certain traditions they had inherited were not based in Scripture and thus were no longer true or necessary in their common life. The practice of paying for indulgences as a means of obtaining forgiveness was ended, clergy were allowed to marry, lay people were encouraged to receive regularly both the bread and wine of the Eucharist once again. In every age the traditions passed on from generation to generation are held up to examination with varying degrees of scrutiny, and we see widespread differences in which traditions are valued and which are set aside in the many churches around the world today.

These differences tend to be influenced by two distinct approaches to the place of Scripture in the church's life that appeared most clearly during the sixteenth-century Reformation. As we have seen, some reformers held that the church should be free to express its faith in a variety of traditions as long as they do not contradict the witness of Scripture. Others believed that only those traditions explicitly affirmed in Scripture should be allowed. Some churches today, for example, do not allow the use of the pipe organ in worship since it is not mentioned in the Bible (it had not yet been invented), while others believe that the musical instruments of any form and age should be used to glorify God, whether they are explicitly mentioned in Scripture or not. The number of the sacraments is a source of contention to this day, with some churches holding only the biblical sacraments of baptism and the Lord's Supper and others believing that the grace of God is also mediated through the rites of marriage, anointing, confirmation, ordination, and reconciliation.

Many other traditions in the worship and prayer of the church have continued to generate controversy and division among the churches in the centuries since the Reformation, and remain the principal differences among denominations today. Most Christians agree on the central tenants of the gospel; it is in the living out of that gospel message that we vary considerably and not always peaceably. The challenge for the church today is to discern which traditions are essential to the revelation of God in Jesus Christ, and which are simply possible expressions of that faith in a particular culture and place. We would do well to follow the example of the early church when, amid tension about whether Gentile converts were required to be circumcised and to follow the Jewish dietary laws, the apostles realized that God had embraced both Jews and Gentiles within the church "by giving them the Holy Spirit, just as he did to us; and in cleansing their hearts by faith he has made no distinction between them and us" (Acts 15:8–9). The leaders of the church therefore decided both Jews and Gentiles were permitted to express their faith in Jesus in their distinctive ways.

REASON AS AN INTERPRETER OF SCRIPTURE

In addition to Scripture and tradition, we also use reason when we seek to learn what is true about God. As human beings we are made in the image of God and have been given the capacity to reason: to think through, discuss, and articulate logical conclusions about the meaning of Scripture and tradition, and their relationship to contemporary concerns and issues. This dialogue is more obviously held among theologians—scholars who study and write about God—but it also takes place in less formal ways, among people who are gathering for worship and study, hearing and preparing sermons, and holding conversations within the local, diocesan, and national churches. It occurs whenever we as a church look at what Scripture and tradition have to teach us and reflect upon how those teachings and experiences of prior generations relate to us in the world in which we live.

It is important to note that although our individual "reasoning" about these concerns is an essential component, it is the *corporate* reasoning of the church that is meant by reason as a third tool of interpretation. Our individual conclusions and ideas must be tested in and shaped by the light of mutual conversation, study, worship, and evaluation. This process of discernment is practiced in every field of knowledge, not just in religious communities, of course, and often the insights learned from other areas of human knowledge have profound ramifications for the religious world.

For example, with the rise of modern scientific theories about evolution and ever-increasing knowledge about the ancient beginnings of the universe, the doctrine of creation has long been a focus for the conflict between literal and more interpretive stances toward the Bible. The controversy has become especially acute in many schools today as science teachers, parents, textbook publishers, and school boards struggle to honor the religious beliefs of students and parents while also being faithful to the insights of modern science. If we take the first chapter of Genesis literally, the Bible would seem to teach that God created everything in six days and then rested on the seventh. Human history would thus have begun with Adam and Eve and their descendants, considerably shortening the timeline for the creation of the Earth and all life. Modern science, on the other hand, posits that the universe is billions of years old and is still in a long process of evolution and ongoing change, with human beings emerging late in the process.

This contrasting understanding of God's work has been the source of reflection and thought for centuries among Christians and scientists of all persuasions. Some Christians take the position that the words of the Bible cannot be wrong, and therefore science must be; others dismiss the biblical version as "a story from a primitive people" and accept only the scientific view as true. Many Christians, on the other hand, take a middle perspective that does not depend on a literalist interpretation of the creation story yet also holds the biblical account to be true in its essential message. We recognize that the story of creation has many forms in the Old Testament, not just the version in the first chapter of Genesis. (See, for example, an alternative story of creation in Genesis 2; see also Psalms 104 and 89, Job 38–39, and Isaiah 45.) We then ask a fundamental question: What is it about God and creation that Scripture is telling us? In the answer to that question we find that the central message of the Bible—that God is the creator of all that is, that this creation is good, that God has a purpose for creation, and that human beings have a pivotal role in that work—is not incompatible with the contemporary scientific theories about creation, evolution, and relativity. Indeed, the discoveries of those in the scientific community are a source of awe and increasing wonder as we see anew the God of the Bible who created this unfathomably enormous and complex universe and pronounced it "good." This is one example of how the church's teachings can change over time, as people of faith reason with and learn from scientists, and conclude that new ways of thinking about the creation of the universe are not necessarily in conflict with the teachings of the Bible.

Reason becomes a powerful means of discernment as the gathered church discusses and debates and draws conclusions about how Scripture and tradition are to be understood in our world today. Sometimes old traditions are upheld for generations, as in the church's celebration of the Eucharist and the continuing practice of baptizing converts to the faith. The Episcopal Church rightly cherishes the prayers, hymns, and liturgical traditions it has received, and it has sought to hold on to those traditions even while updating or reforming its worship in the light of new understandings of the church's history. Sometimes new teachings and traditions come from this use of reason by the whole church, as when churches reevaluate their practice of excluding women from their ordained ministries in response to new insights emerging from Scripture and other ancient texts about the important roles of women in the earliest Christian communities. Many churches have likewise revised their prayer books and liturgies to incorporate newly recovered prayers and practices from the earliest centuries of the church's life, and to include contemporary images and ideas in their worship services.

Changes large and small are almost always accompanied by tension and conflict, and at such times it is helpful for us to remember the wisdom offered in the biblical accounts of similar conflicts within communities of faith. Very soon after the death and resurrection of Jesus, as the first Christians were struggling to interpret and express their experience of Jesus as the Messiah of God, the apostles were subjected to violent persecution at the hands of the religious authorities of their day. One of those leaders, a Pharisee named Gamaliel, urged his fellow council members to be patient with the radical innovations of these followers of the Way. "If this plan or this undertaking is of human origin, it will fail," he told them, "but if it is of God, you will not be able to overthrow them—in that case you may even be found fighting against God!" (Acts 5:38–39). We can gain confidence in the process of change by practicing a similar patience: if the proposed new practices withstand the test of time, they will be incorporated into the tradition of the church passed on to future generations, but if they are not worthy of the revelation of God in Scripture, shaped by centuries of tradition and informed by reason, they will usually fade away or be tossed out by future reformers.

THE BIBLE'S AUTHORITY TODAY

So, with this body of biblical interpretation over the centuries, mediated by reason and tradition, what can we conclude about the Bible's authority for the church today? How does this "three-legged stool" help us know what power the Bible has to shape our lives? In our pluralistic society, where many of the traditional authorities by which our life and behavior were once governed have been questioned and religious regulations are now seen as a matter of personal choice, how can the Bible be a unifying authority within the church?

While individual Christians may vary in their submission to and understanding of biblical authority, for the Christian church as a whole, the message and meaning of the Bible is (or is intended to be) at the heart of decision-making and teaching. What we call "the word of God" exercises great influence and guidance for the life and practice of the "people of God," although the ways in which that influence is felt—the ways the Bible regulates the church's life and practice—changes and adapts to the times. Many of the "renewal movements" in the life of the church have been inspired by a desire to center the life of the church on a specific interpretation of biblical teachings and designs. For example, the movement started by Francis of Assisi in the late Middle Ages was based on a more literal reading of the message of Jesus to "sell your possessions, and give the money to the poor, . . . then come, follow me" (Matthew 19:21) than was usually practiced by the church at that time. St. Francis began his ministry outside the official structures of the church and its teachings, but eventually his way of life was widely received by people in the official church structures who recognized the biblical authority of their embrace of poverty.

Clearly, the historical and cultural situation of the church has an enormous impact on how biblical authority is exercised in the church. We have noted that during the Reformation those who sought to change the church wanted to make it more faithful to the Bible. This "back to the Bible" movement was fueled by the development of the printing press as the Bible, which had previously been known primarily through worship in church, was now available to anyone who could read. The printing press was also a means for those reformers who were critical of the church to spread their message widely. All of this change in the social and political structures of the culture led to a breakdown of the old authorities and a need for new authorities to take their place. For many of the reformers and their followers, the Bible filled this need: the Scriptures (or, more accurately, each reformer's particular interpretation of the Scriptures) became their "authority" and the basis for the formation of new church communities and national identities.

Now, in our modern and postmodern time, a similar situation has presented itself. The authority of institutions, be they political, educational, or religious, is being challenged, and new sources of authority are emerging. The idea of a "back to the Bible" movement is attractive to many, because it seems to be grounded in history and to offer very clear solutions to the kinds of moral and philosophical dilemmas posed by our complex and pluralistic world. But for others the idea that one book—and an old one at that, written without the insights of modern science, without the experience of modern technology, with no apparent connection to the contemporary world—might have authority to determine the shape of their lives seems ridiculous. They would question how a book that depended on the experience and knowledge of people who lived many thousands of years ago could possibly give authoritative guidance and direction for people today, especially about complex contemporary issues such as stem cell research and nuclear weapons.

Anglicans today hold both ends of these perspectives and all variations in between, especially during these times of increasing polarization within the church. Yet most Anglicans do agree that the word of God is a *living* word: it was not written down centuries ago as a fossilized "word for all time," but rather is to be lived and reengaged in every age. As life and knowledge and history unfold, the meaning of those Scriptures takes on new life and purpose in light of the ways God is being revealed in our specific age. And so, the church is always in a living, active conversation with the Bible about its direction and meaning for the church today. We are a church who believes in an incarnate Lord, a God who became one of us, a God who is interested and intimately involved in the day-to-day life of every person. We seek by prayer, conversation, and study to reach a consensus within the church as to how we are to be led by Scripture to address the very real and pressing concerns, issues, and needs of the world in which we live today.

As an example, we could consider the fact that over the past century history has shown the increasingly devastating human cost of warfare. The rise of modern weaponry has made war, once a common tool of statecraft, a problematic issue for our society. We have seen in the last one hundred years the most catastrophic wars ever, and wars now affect civilian populations as much as, if not more than, the soldiers in the opposing armies. In countries throughout the world significant peace movements have emerged, many of them supported and led by pacifist Christians. At the same time, there are also a significant number of Christians who still believe warfare to be an appropriate tool for nations to use, both to defend themselves and also to impose their will on others.

Some of these peace movements have their roots in the pacifist teachings of the so-called peace churches, such as the Society of Friends (Quakers) and the Church of the Brethren. Members of these churches have been permitted a "conscientious objection" to armed service in combat, based on those teachings. These churches have stood in opposition to all of the wars of the twentieth century and their members have refused induction and service, or have agreed to serve in noncombatant roles in those wars.

In the Episcopal Church, the debate over war and peace began in earnest during the 1960s and 70s, in the heat of the Vietnam War. Looking to the Scriptures for guidance on this issue, some saw in Jesus' teachings in the Sermon on the Mount (Matthew 5–7), especially those about turning the other cheek and loving the enemy (5:38–48), a call to absolute pacifism. But others found passages in the New Testament and the Hebrew Scriptures that seemed to justify warfare: Jesus' words about war in some of his parables (Luke 14:31–33) and his violent cleansing of the temple, God's war against Satan in the book of Revelation, and the depiction of the God of Israel as a warrior god led them to conclude that the Scriptures do not oppose war, as such. Coupled with both Jesus and Paul's strong support of governing authorities, these and similar passages seemed to make a case for letting governments make the decisions about war and peace, and leaving religious convictions out of it.

In this situation, a literal reading of the Bible could be seen to support either position. So how should the conflict be resolved? A long-standing teaching of the church known as the *just war theory* offered some help. This teaching, developed originally by Augustine of Hippo in the fourth century and modified by others over time, suggested that war was sometimes a necessity and was therefore morally acceptable, but that certain conditions needed to be met if Christians were to support it. Some of these conditions included that the war be initiated by a legitimate government; that it be for a "just" cause; and that it not significantly involve noncombatants. This gave many Christians a moral stance from which to examine specific wars or conflicts.

Yet even among Christians who accept the just war theory, differences of interpretation can arise. Some have argued that in an age of nuclear weapons, where entire populations of cities and even countries could be obliterated, war can no longer be tolerated as a moral means for resolving international conflicts. Others have claimed that a "limited" war can be a means by which nations respond to intolerable offenses by other nations. So, while the just war theory offers some measure of interpretation of the Scripture's teaching on warfare, it does not fully resolve the issue. It did, however, allow the Episcopal Church to oppose the Vietnam War at its General Conventions in 1970 and 1973, on the basis of its cruelty and failure to distinguish between civilians and combatants. It has also provided the moral theological support for leaders of the Episcopal Church to speak out against the use of force in several incidents since that time, especially the Gulf War and Operation Desert Storm. These reasoned and corporately discussed concerns took both Scripture and the just war tradition and interpreted them to fit the situation in which the nation found itself in these wars.

In its stance toward war and in all other moral questions of our time, in order for the Bible to have authority for the church, the church must be willing to submit to that authority. When agreement on the boundaries and nature of that submission is not shared by all, the church must engage in working to bring about consensus. These conversations and studies often take a very long time. It took nearly five hundred years for the church to reach a consensus of sorts on the creeds, and many more years before the beliefs expressed by those creeds were embraced by most Christians. We are still trying, after nearly six hundred years, to work through the disagreements brought about during the Reformation. And today new tensions emerge daily, as various parties to the conversation threaten to leave the Anglican Communion in order to form a church they believe to be more in line with the teachings of the Bible as they understand them. These are tense and polarized times, and sometimes it is very difficult for people to wait patiently for a consensus to emerge.[15] In the meantime, the church is vulnerable to misunderstanding, confusion, vacillation, and accusations of being "wishy-washy" toward all biblical authority. As the issue is worked through, the church can and does come to conclusions that are authoritative and firm—such as its decisions affirming the leadership roles of women, for example—but those conclusions can take decades or even centuries to evolve.

No matter what the particular controversy embroiling the church in a particular time and place, the fundamental embrace of the Bible as inspired or "filled with Spirit" informs Anglican approaches to Scripture at their best. Anglicans therefore believe the best place for the authority of the Bible to be experienced is in the context of the community gathered for worship, where the Spirit of God is present and lively among us. The words and images of the Bible have permeated our liturgies from the beginning, and it is to the presence of the Bible in the Book of Common Prayer that we now turn.

QUESTIONS FOR REFLECTION AND DISCUSSION

1. In what ways do you read the Bible? For information? For inspiration? For a better understanding of God's work and word? As a prayer? What place does interpretation play in your understanding of the Bible?

2. How would you describe the authority the Bible has in your congregation? In your denomination? Where and how do you see that authority expressed and lived out?

3. What authority does the Bible have in your own life? In what ways have you chosen to live differently because of your interpretation of the words of the Bible?

4. How do we make choices about which parts of the Bible are relevant to our world and the issues that we deal with in the political and social controversies of our time? How does the Bible inform and shape our common life?

The Bible in the Prayer Book

When you walk through the doors of your local library, you may see hundreds, perhaps thousands of books lining the shelves. How do you even begin to choose a book to read? If you are interested in a particular topic or author, you might head first for the card catalog or library database. Or perhaps you simply want a good novel or an interesting biography, and you go to those sections to browse the shelves. Once you've selected a book, again you have choices: you can read the back cover and endorsements first, perhaps even find a review or summary. You might skip the preface and head straight for chapter one. You might turn to the glossy photographs and illustrations in the middle before reading the text. If it is a collection of short stories or essays you might peruse the table of contents and choose one that sparks your interest. Or you might simply start on the very first page and move page by page through the text.

The Bible is a whole library in one volume, and just as there are many ways to read a novel or a collection of short stories, there are countless ways to read the books of the Bible. You can start on page one and read straight through, from Genesis to Revelation. You can choose a particular author (Paul, for example) and read everything that author wrote. Or you can choose a certain book or part of a book—the book of Job perhaps, or the stories of Jesus' birth in Matthew and Luke—and start there. When you are reading the

Bible on your own at home, you will want to try a variety of methods because each provides unique insights. Reading through the entire Gospel of Mark in one sitting, for example, will give you a compelling, broad-brush view of Jesus' ministry. Taking one of the parables Mark tells, or even a single saying of Jesus, and focusing on it—studying the meaning of the words, reading commentaries, praying the text, letting it sink in, and ruminating on it for some time—yields a different but equally fruitful understanding.

What if the book you chose at the library is a selection you're reading for your book club or reading group? When you gather with other people who have read that book, what happens when you hear passages read aloud? Perhaps you remember the passage well and were also struck by it, and you are eager to share your insights. Or perhaps you didn't get that far in your reading, or you found the passage confusing or offensive. You might find the comments shared by your fellow group members helpful or irritating; perhaps their interpretations vary markedly from your own, or perhaps they fill in some gap, just as your comments add to the general understanding of the group.

Hearing the Bible in church is in many ways like that reading group. People of all religious traditions have long gathered to hear their Scriptures read aloud, to hear their unique story of how God has come to them told and retold. They gather to deepen their understanding through the interpretations offered by others, even—or especially—when those interpretations differ. Just as in a reading group, sometimes the parts of the Bible one person finds boring are intriguing to another; teachings offered by a biblical scholar or preacher might shed light on a passage that seems confusing or strange without an understanding of the context; a verse that seems meaningless to one reader might be the source of tremendous comfort and insight for another. For Christians, this telling of our religious story happens every time we gather for prayer and worship on Sundays and throughout the days of the week. Whether it is a single verse or several lengthy passages, reading the Bible is almost always part of our worship and prayer.

In addition to hearing passages read from the Bible, worshipers encounter the Bible all through the worship experience. The prayers, hymns, and other words that make up worship are often direct quotations from the Bible. When they are not, they are regularly paraphrases of biblical passages or themes. This is true in the worship of most synagogues and churches, and it is also true in the Episcopal Church. The prayers and forms of worship set forth in the Book of Common Prayer are thoroughly and often explicitly grounded in the Scriptures. As one bishop in the nineteenth century put it:

> [The Book of Common Prayer] was composed principally out of Scripture, or out of ancient liturgies and fathers. Even where entire parts of Scripture or of the fathers are not taken or applied, yet their spirit and manner, their style and character are still preserved.[16]

Scripture in Episcopal Worship

If we look at the forms for worship in the 1979 Book of Common Prayer, we can see this principle of biblical reference at work. The first major section of liturgies in the Prayer Book includes the rites for the Daily Office. These orders for daily prayer in the morning, at noon, in the evening, and at the end of the day consist almost exclusively of scriptural texts. The opening sentences, canticles, psalms, lessons, and prayers all either explicitly quote the Bible or are based upon biblical phrases. Sometimes the quotations give the chapter and verse in the Bible where the passage may be found; the opening sentences and many of the canticles provide such citations. In other instances the biblical phrases are not identified specifically, but the imagery and phrases are taken from a variety of passages.

Consider the service of Morning Prayer, for example. If you open your Prayer Book to the Rite Two version (page 75), you will immediately see four pages of Scripture verses, from which the officiant selects "one or more" to begin the service. The confession of sin follows, which is a practice urged in the New Testament, such as in the letter of James: "Confess your sins to one another, and pray for one another, so that you may be healed" (5:16). A number of psalms are then read, beginning with either the *Venite* (Psalm 95) or the *Jubilate* (Psalm 100)—or, during Easter Week, the *Pascha nostrum* (Christ our Passover) is read, which is a combination of two passages from 1 Corinthians and one from Romans.

The reading of the Scripture lessons for the day follows the Psalms, interspersed with the reading or singing of canticles— nearly all of which are themselves passages from the Bible. The 1979 Prayer Book greatly expanded the number of these canticles available for regular use, and in other prayer books recently revised throughout the world an even greater abundance can be found.

The Apostles' Creed that follows the canticles is among the most ancient statements of belief in the church, and was probably part of the affirmation of faith made by the candidates at baptism. It tells in simple statements the entire story of the New Testament and what those early Christians came to believe about who God is: the Father almighty who created heaven and earth, Jesus the Son of God who died and rose again, and the Holy Spirit who dwells in the church as the communion of saints.

The prayers offered after the creed include the Lord's Prayer; according to the gospels of Matthew and Luke, this is the prayer Jesus taught his disciples when they asked him to teach them to pray. Though he may have been giving them a simple outline of intentions rather than actual words to repeat, from its beginnings the church has cherished this prayer and in its repetition has tried to pray more nearly as Jesus desired.

The sentences that follow are called *suffrages*: the person leading Morning Prayer says the first line and the people respond with the second. They are all verses from the Psalms, compiled into a format of prayer for congregational use. The first set, for example, "Show us your mercy, O Lord; / And grant us your salvation," is Psalm 85:7 (BCP); the second, "Clothe your ministers with righteousness; / Let your people sing with joy," is Psalm 132:9 (BCP). Thus in these prayers Christians share in the more ancient words of the Psalms, the "prayer book" of the Hebrew Scriptures.

The prayers said after the suffrages in Morning Prayer are called *collects*, and although some date from the early and medieval church, a number were written or revised at the time the first Book of Common Prayer in English was compiled or later. In all of them we can see the images and words of Scripture. The Collect for Saturdays, for example, was written by Edward Benson, who was Archbishop of Canterbury in the late nineteenth century:

> Almighty God, who after the creation of the world rested from all your works and sanctified a day of rest for all your creatures: Grant that we, putting away all earthly anxieties, may be duly prepared for the service of your sanctuary, and that our rest here upon earth may be a preparation for the eternal rest promised to your people in heaven; through Jesus Christ our Lord. Amen. (BCP 99)

In this prayer we hear echoes of the creation story in Genesis, in which God "blessed the seventh day and hallowed it, because on it God rested from all the work that he had done in creation" (Genesis 2:3). We also hear the words of Jesus in his Sermon on the Mount, when he urges his followers not to worry about earthly things, what they will eat or what they will wear, for God "knows that you need all these things. But strive first for the kingdom of God and his righteousness, and all these things will be given to you as well" (Matthew 6:32–33). In chapter four of the letter to the Hebrews, we find the source for the allusion to "the eternal rest promised to your people in heaven" in that author's discussion of God's promise of rest to his people in the promised land.

Finally, the General Thanksgiving that gathers up all the prayers is likewise chock-full of the words and images of the Bible, from the memorable phrase describing the Christ's presence in us as "the hope of glory" in Colossians 1:27 to Zechariah's song recalling God's merciful faithfulness to his people, so that we "might serve him without fear, in holiness and righteousness before him all our days" (Luke 1:74–75). The service of Morning Prayer then concludes with the reading of a verse from Scripture, just as it began.

Like the rites for the daily offices, the collects appointed for each Sunday and for other holy days and special occasions also contain phrases and quotations from the Bible, mostly from the New Testament, or they are prayers used in the church's life over the centuries and thus contain allusions to other Christian writings as well.

The collect for the Confession of Saint Peter (BCP 238) recalls Peter's affirmation of "Jesus as Messiah and Son of the living God" and asks God to keep the church "steadfast upon the rock of this faith"—a direct reference to Jesus' words to his disciple Simon, "And I tell you, you are Peter [Greek: *Petros*], and on this rock [Greek: *petra*] I will build my church" (Matthew 16:18). Sometimes we can see subtle changes in the church's theology over the centuries in the revisions of these collects, based on which stories in Scripture the church is finding most meaningful at that time in its history. The collect in the 1549 Book of Common Prayer for the feast of Saint Mary Magdalene, for example, focused on the scriptural image of her as a woman of many sins, and our common need for repentance:

> Merciful Father, give us grace, that we never presume to sin through the example of any creature; but if it shall chance us at any time to offend thy divine majesty; that then we may truly repent, and lament the same, after the example of Mary Magdalene, and by lively faith obtain remission of all our sins.[17]

The revised collect we have today focuses rather on Mary's restoration to health and her status as an apostolic witness to the resurrection:

> Almighty God, whose blessed Son restored Mary Magdalene to health of body and of mind, and called her to be a witness of his resurrection: Mercifully grant that by your grace we may be healed from all our infirmities and know you in the power of his unending life. (BCP 242)

The liturgies for Holy Week in the 1979 Prayer Book also utilize large portions of Scripture, from our echoing on Palm Sunday the pilgrims on the road to Jerusalem who shouted, "Blessed is he who comes in the name of the Lord, Hosanna in the highest," through the reenactment of Jesus' washing of the disciples' feet on Maundy Thursday and the reading of the Passion Gospel on

Good Friday. Holy Week culminates in the Easter Vigil, with its series of lengthy readings from the Bible outlining the history of salvation, accompanied by collects that offer praise to God for the creation and redemption of the world (see BCP 288–291).

Other forms for worship and prayer in the Book of Common Prayer contain similar echoes and references to Bible. There can hardly be a more powerful and memorable opening to the rite for burial, for example, than the blending of Jesus' reassurance of eternal life, the confident words of Job that were spoken in the midst of desolation, and the passage from the letter to the Romans affirming our home in Christ. These readings are recited at the beginning of the church service, often during the procession bearing the body of the person who has died:

> I am the resurrection and the life, saith the Lord;
> he that believeth in me, though he were dead, yet shall
>   he live;
> and whosoever liveth and believeth in me shall never die.
>   [John 11:25–26]

> I know that my Redeemer liveth,
> and that he shall stand at the latter day upon the earth;
> and though this body be destroyed, yet shall I see God;
> whom I shall see for myself and mine eyes shall behold,
> and not as a stranger. [Job 19:25–27]

> For none of us liveth to himself,
> and no man dieth to himself.
> For if we live, we live unto the Lord;
> and if we die, we die unto the Lord.
> Whether we live, therefore, or die, we are the Lord's.
>   [Romans 14:7–8] (BCP 469)

As with the rites of the daily office and the pastoral offices, the forms for the celebration of the Holy Eucharist—perhaps the most frequently used liturgies in the Prayer Book—are full of biblical allusions, especially in the prayers of the people, the confession, and the prayers of the Great Thanksgiving. Even the Nicene Creed, although not a biblical passage, uses phrases and images from the Scriptures, as it defines the faith of the church. Because several of the alternatives for the Great Thanksgiving in our Book of Common Prayer are grounded in ancient prayers from the early church, they echo the Jewish blessings over bread and wine offered at mealtimes, and thus contain imagery from both the Hebrew and Christian Scriptures. The opening sentence, "The Lord be with you," is taken from Boaz's greeting to the reapers in Ruth 2:4, for example, and the first two lines of the *Sanctus*—"Holy, holy, holy Lord, God of power and might, heaven and earth are full of your glory"—are a paraphrase of Isaiah 6:3.

Each of the Eucharistic Prayers contains paragraphs called the Words of Institution, which are a compilation of the New Testament passages in the gospels and 1 Corinthians describing the Last Supper and the Eucharist of the early church. In these often repeated words, we learn that Jesus "took bread; and when he had given thanks to you, he broke it, and gave it to his disciples, and said, 'Take, eat: This is my Body, which is given for you. Do this for the remembrance of me'" (BCP 362). In these and many other prayers of the Eucharist, we hear the words and images of the Bible in our worship each Sunday, even though we may not always realize their origin in Scripture.

In addition to the prayers and liturgies found in the Book of Common Prayer, worship in the Episcopal Church includes singing, and many of the hymns of the church are also biblical in origin. Many hymns are metrical versions of the Psalms (for example, Hymn 645 in *The Hymnal 1982* is a paraphrase of the familiar Psalm 23) and others are paraphrases of other scriptural passages (for example, Hymn 417 is a paraphrase of Revelation 5:12–13).[18] Most hymns contain allusions to the Bible and biblical themes, even when they do not directly quote or paraphrase a passage.

The familiar hymn "Rock of Ages" offers a good example of how hymn writers use biblical passages and images to create a musical expression of our faith. The first verse of this eighteenth-century hymn reads:

Rock of ages, cleft for me,
let me hide myself in thee;
let the water and the blood
from thy wounded side that flowed,
be of sin the double cure,
cleanse me from its guilt and power.[19]

The word "rock" is used in several ways in the Scriptures. It is an image for God, as in Psalm 18:2, 42:9, and Deuteronomy 32:4. The rock that is broken, or cleft, in the hymn, however, seems to refer to the rock that Moses struck in the wilderness (Exodus 17; Numbers 20), from which water poured out for the thirsty Israelites. Further, it is a reference to Christ who is the Rock (1 Corinthians 10:4) and who was broken for our sins.

From the very first phrase, a medley of biblical ideas and images emerge in this hymn. Hiding in the cleft of a rock is a means of protection (see Exodus 33:22 and 1 Kings 19), but it can also mean safety in the "bosom" of God. The image of water and blood refers to the Passover in Exodus, but also to Jesus' shedding of water and blood on the cross (John 19:34). The reference to Jesus becomes explicit in the words "from thy wounded side"; the use of the pronoun "thy" at this point clarifies that the hymn is intended as a prayer to Jesus. The hymn's first verse concludes with references to curing sin (see Mark 2:1–11, 17) and cleansing from sin and guilt (see Jeremiah 33:8; 1 John 1:7, 9). This kind of working with and weaving texts together in a way that creates multiple images is common in many hymns. And it helps us see why knowing something of the Bible can be of great help in entering into the worship and praise of the church's liturgy.

In a well-planned liturgy you can often find hymns that reflect the biblical passages that have been (or will be) read during the service. This allows the texts to be "heard" in a variety of ways— both in their literal form, as they are read, and then in a more artistic form, as the texts are mingled with other images in the hymns. If the stained glass and art in a church also reflect the texts being read, what a wonderful opportunity to allow the Bible to speak to one's heart and one's imagination!

So, in addition to hearing some specific passages of the Bible read in worship, people in the congregation are hearing the words and the thoughts of the Bible throughout the worship experience. While we may not know the entire Bible as a book, we may well know more biblical phrases and ideas than we realize, simply because we have heard them repeated week after week, year after year in the church's worship services.

The Lectionary

In the Episcopal Church, as in many other liturgical churches and religious traditions, readings from the Scriptures are taken from a lectionary—a list that divides the Bible into selected passages to be read over a specific period of time (in most cases, three years). We have two lectionaries in our Prayer Book: a Daily Office Lectionary that provides selections for Morning and Evening Prayer (BCP 934–1001) and a Lectionary for Sundays (BCP 888–931). The Sunday lectionary also includes readings (called *Propers*) for holy days, saints' days, various occasions (such as a church convention), and specific topics (such as social justice or education). The overall purpose of both lectionaries is to give Episcopalians a broad exposure to a large portion of the Bible over the course of two or three years, rather than limiting those readings to just the passages that are most appealing to us, or that simply reinforce perhaps inadequate understandings of our faith we nonetheless find comforting. The Episcopal Church's lectionaries were based on an ecumenical lectionary developed in the 1970s and was used by many Christian denominations. A newer draft, called *The Revised Common Lectionary*, may now be used in place of the lectionaries in the Book of Common Prayer, and soon will be used as the authorized lectionary in the Episcopal Church in place of the one in the Book of Common Prayer.

In these lectionaries, readings are provided from each of the major sections of the Bible, and are divided into a three-year cycle. Each year is identified by a letter: Year A, Year B, and Year C. The year can usually be found somewhere in your service leaflet, but you can also use the formula for determining which cycle is being read on page 888 of the 1979 Book of Common Prayer. Each year has a slightly different "flavor" and theme, usually based on the gospel that is being read that year: Matthew in Year A, Mark in Year B, and Luke in Year C, with readings from the gospel of John interspersed throughout, especially during Lent and Easter.

The first lesson (sometimes called the Old Testament reading) is chosen from one of the various books of the Hebrew Scriptures: the reading for the First Sunday of Advent in Year A, for example, is Isaiah 2:1–5; other first readings in Year A include passages from Exodus, Jeremiah, Leviticus, and Joel. A selection from the book of Psalms is also provided: these hymns and prayers of ancient Israel remain part of the song and prayer of the church, and the texts are often prayed or chanted by the entire congregation, or sung by a choir. There are two readings from the New Testament: a selection from one of the letters of the apostles or early church communities, usually called the epistle, and a reading from one of the four gospels. The second reading on the First Sunday of Advent in Year A is from Paul's letter to the Romans, for example, and the gospel is a passage from Matthew. The Prayer Book rubrics allow flexibility in the lessons for a particular service, both in their length and how many are chosen, but the gospel must always be read.

The readings are selected in two ways. During the seasons of the church year (Advent, Christmas, Lent, and Easter), lessons are selected based upon the themes of the season.[20] On those Sundays it is usually possible to discern a thematic connection to the gospel passage among some if not all of the readings. An obvious example would be the readings for Maundy Thursday (which are the same for all three years): the first reading is the story in Exodus of the first Passover; the Psalm tells of God giving manna from heaven to the Israelites in the wilderness; the New Testament lesson is Paul's version of the Last Supper described in his first letter to the Corinthian church; and the gospel reading is either John's description of Jesus washing his disciples' feet before the Last Supper or Luke's story of the meal shared at the Last Supper. During other times of the year, especially the weeks "after Epiphany" and "after Pentecost" (often called "Ordinary Time"), the lessons often follow a specific book in sequence, so that over the course of several weeks the entire content of a single book may be heard. You will usually not be able to see a single overarching theme among the readings on those Sundays because each reading stands alone in its own particular context. On these Sundays it is especially helpful to have some background knowledge of the type, style, author, and history of the book being read.

Since the readings from the Hebrew Scriptures are selected from a much larger collection of writings than the New Testament (the Old Testament has thirty-nine books, or fifty-four if the Apocrypha is included, compared to twenty-seven much shorter books in the New Testament), only a small portion of the Old Testament books will be read on Sundays. The readings from the Hebrew Scriptures are taken from all the major sections and most of the books of the collection. They are selected for their liturgical relevance during the seasons of the church year, and for their connection to the gospel reading during the remaining Sundays of the year. In the *Revised Common Lectionary* the Ordinary Time readings are taken from a specific book and read in sequence over a period of several weeks. You may want to ask the clergy of your congregation which lectionary your parish currently follows and why that lectionary was chosen.

One book of the Hebrew Scriptures is read almost in its entirety in Christian churches, however, and usually a passage is chosen every Sunday: the book of Psalms. These hymns or poems were written for use in the temple rituals of the kings and people of Israel, and are traditionally called the Psalms of David (the great king of Israel in the tenth century BCE), although most were probably not written directly by him. The Psalms seem to have been especially important to Jesus' spiritual life: he often quoted or referred to a psalm at significant moments. Like the other readings, the psalm is usually connected to a theme of the day, or to one of the other readings. It is usually not read by a single reader, however, but is recited or sung (sometimes antiphonally and sometimes in unison) by the congregation or a choir.

The second reading is taken from the letters (often called *epistles*, from the old English word for correspondence) and other writings of the Christian Scriptures. The Acts of the Apostles, written by the gospel writer Luke, details the early history of the church, especially the journeys of the apostle Paul. Of the twenty-one letters in the New Testament, thirteen are called "letters of Paul," with others attributed to various apostles and their companions. One, the letter to the Hebrews, is without a named author. Like the readings from the Hebrew Scriptures, readings from the New Testament epistles and writings are selected either to accent a seasonal theme, or to read through a single letter in course, week by week.

In Christian worship, the gospel reading is usually the most important (and it is therefore read last, no matter how many readings are included in a particular service). Each of the four gospels tells the story of Jesus' life, ministry, teaching, death, and resurrection from the different perspectives of the various church communities that grew in the decades following Jesus' death. They were written by people who either knew Jesus or who heard the stories from people who were eyewitnesses to the events, and they share marked similarities as well as startling differences. Matthew, Mark, and Luke (the synoptic gospels) describe a number of the same events, tell many of the same stories, and have a generally similar outline for the life of Jesus. John, the fourth gospel, offers a different perspective, but does include some of the episodes depicted in the other gospels. The gospels are not comprehensive "biographies" of Jesus, nor are they "objective" historical documents; rather, they were written to tell people about the good news of Jesus, whom they believed to be the Messiah and Savior of the world. Thus, the place of the gospel reading in the church's worship is to announce "good news" to the people of the congregation so that their faith in Jesus as their Lord and Savior can be strengthened (which is why it is read by the deacon, celebrant, or another priest, as part of their vocation to proclaim and interpret the gospel to the people).

INTERPRETING THE BIBLE IN WORSHIP

Encountering the Bible in the worship service can present some difficulties for those who are not very familiar with Scripture. Because the readings are usually fairly short snippets it may not be clear why they are being read, or how they fit with the rest of the story, or how they relate to one another—if, in fact, they do.

Because they are read out of their context in the book of the Bible from which they are taken, as if they were "stand alone" elements, the meaning of these passages can be obscured if we are not familiar with the rest of the book or letter. Even when the readings are taken from a single book or letter in sequence over several weeks, because of the long time period between hearings (usually at least a week), the connections between readings are not easy to make. So in the church's liturgy there are a number of interpretive aids to help us understand the Scriptures being read.

The most common interpretive aid you will encounter on Sunday mornings is the separate leaflet containing the readings for that service; these leaflets are usually inserted into the service bulletin. They can be helpful for those who prefer to read *and* hear the lessons at the same time, and who find the visual reinforcement useful. They can also be taken home for further reflection and study. On the other hand, the leaflets do not provide any information about the context of the passages, which would reveal something of their meaning, and all the readings for the three-year cycle are generally taken from the same translation of the Bible. It may be a good idea, then, to follow the Sunday readings in a Bible from a different translation as they are being read, or to take the leaflet home and look up the passages in your Bible there, reading the chapters or stories that come before and after each lesson, comparing translations, and learning more about who wrote that book and why. Many people find it more profitable to locate the readings in the lectionary for the upcoming Sunday during the week before, and to do their study in preparation for hearing the lessons read aloud in the context of corporate worship.

In many parishes, before reading the lessons the lay readers begin with a brief introduction that gives the context for the passage and summarizes its content. A variety of these introductory materials is available today, and they can be quite useful in providing background information that helps us understand the passage being read. It is important, though, to realize that these books, too, are offering a particular interpretation of the Bible through the words they choose to summarize the content, and the meaning they attribute to whatever content they choose to highlight. An introductory preface to one of the gospel stories concerning the birth of Jesus, for example, could speak in terms of a historical event with a focus on the visitations from angels and magi, or the introduction could describe the stories as wondrous myths whose truths lie more in their meaning as a fulfillment of God's promise to send a savior to Israel than in their factual basis. Whenever you hear a description of what the Bible says or means, you should ask yourself what might be the interpretive stance of the description's author, and what other interpretations might be possible. Since it is important not to allow these interpretive aids to become a substitute for your own sense of what is being read, you need to listen more closely to the text than to the introduction.

It should also be noted that lectionaries themselves are a means by which the Bible is interpreted in worship, through the choices made about which passages are to be read in church and when they are to be read. A number of these choices are simply taken from long-standing traditional readings for certain days, like Christmas and Easter, that has continued from the early and medieval church through the first Book of Common Prayer in 1549 and on through subsequent revisions of the Prayer Book. But lectionaries have also changed over the years, and those who select the readings are influenced by their theological, social, and cultural assumptions and preconceptions. Portions of the Bible that seem old-fashioned, out of date, too negative or theologically problematic, or simply "politically incorrect" to a particular age or culture, such as verses referring to women being silent in church or God's calling the Israelites to practice genocide, or psalms that yearn for the dashing of children against rocks, are sometimes left out of the selections to be read in public worship. The readings chosen for worship are a good way to come to know what parts of Scripture are important in the teaching and worship of the church, but these readings are intended primarily to invite us into a deeper relationship with the Bible and with God, and it is important not to dismiss the portions that are not read in worship when you are reading and studying the Bible at home or with others. These "troublesome" passages often have a great deal to teach us about who God is or was perceived to be, how people in previous generations have encountered and envisioned God, and who we are in relationship with God and other people.

Another interpretive aid to the Bible we have in worship are the hymns, anthems, and service music. As mentioned earlier, these musical elements of the service are often chosen to express the themes of that particular Sunday, and the words of many of the hymns in *The Hymnal 1982* retell the stories of the Bible by paraphrasing the words of Scripture, if they are not exact quotations. But they also add an interpretive element. The African American spiritual "Were You There When They Crucified My Lord?" (Hymn 172), for example, takes each element of the crucifixion story told in the gospels and brings home the emotional horror of that event for those who stood by watching Jesus suffer: "Sometimes it causes me to tremble, tremble, tremble." The hymns for evening often include praise for the Creator of the light and all living beings, thus recalling the story of creation in Genesis:

> O blest Creator, source of light,
> you gave the day with splendor bright,
> when on the new and living earth
> you brought all things to glorious birth. (Hymn 28)

Many other hymns also express through poetic verse a particular story or image found in the Bible in such a way as to communicate not just the words, but an interpretive meaning that the poet or musician wants to get across.

Likewise, the words to the musical elements of the service itself are often passages directly from Scripture that have been strung together into a single musical element. The *Gloria in excelsis*, which is often sung at the beginning of the Eucharist, is a good example of this (see BCP 356, and S 273 in *The Hymnal 1982*). In that text you will find echoes from a number of Scripture verses, from the song of the angels extolling the birth of Jesus (Luke 2:14) to the words of John the Baptist at the baptism of Jesus, "the Lamb of God who takes away the sin of the world" (John 1:29). The very name "Lamb of God" is an allusion to the Passover lamb sacrificed by the Israelites in the Hebrew Scriptures. Thus in this and countless other places we see ways that the church links the images and theology of the Old and New Testaments in its worship and life of prayer, with the Scriptures of the Hebrew and Christian communities interpreting each other.

As we have seen, even the texts and prayers of the Episcopal liturgies are an interpretation of the Bible. A great many of the words in our 1979 Book of Common Prayer were taken from the earlier prayer books of the Reformation, which in turn were either taken from or shaped by the words and prayers of the Latin Mass of the medieval church. The early prayer books of the church were likewise replete with the words of Scripture, as the biblical scholar Jaroslav Pelikan observes:

> The Vulgate was the Bible of Europe for over a thousand years, and it was the mother lode of the Latin Mass. Those who, from the perspective of the Protestant Reformation with its doctrine of "the Bible only," criticize the Middle Ages for having neglected the study of the Bible should examine the text of the Latin Mass with a concordance to the Vulgate in hand. Phrase by phrase, sometimes word by single word, it is a daisy chain of biblical quotations.[21]

In the Liturgy, the Scriptures were thus a way of clarifying and supporting the theological claims of the church. As prayer books were revised and edited and written following the Reformation, the tradition of using the words and images of the Bible in this way continued, and became one of the ways the Reformation churches and the Roman Catholic churches used the Bible to refute and negate the claims of the other.

It is an interesting and informative exercise to try to discover the biblical sources of the words of our 1979 Book of Common Prayer, both the prayers and texts that are new to this Prayer Book and those that have come down to us from the church's tradition. Or, you might also want to see if you can find the sources in the Bible for your favorite hymns. The echoes become easier to hear as you become more familiar with the texts of the Bible.

Sermons as Biblical Interpretation

In the synagogues and gatherings of Jewish believers, the reading of the Hebrew Scriptures has long been followed by an exposition and interpretation of what the passages mean. Jesus himself participated in this tradition when he attended synagogue services in Nazareth, read a passage from the prophet Isaiah, and began his homily with the startling and not altogether popular assertion that "today this scripture has been fulfilled in your hearing" (Luke 4:16–30). The early church adopted this pattern of following the reading of Scripture with a sermon as well, and while it fell into disuse in many places during the Middle Ages because illiterate clergy were not always capable of delivering them coherently, the custom of having a sermon or homily at some point during Sunday worship was reinvigorated during the Reformation—often to the point that it overshadowed all else in the service. In our Prayer Book the sermon has been restored to its earlier place immediately following the reading of the lessons from the Bible, emphasizing its primary purpose as an interpretation of those readings.

The sermon is among the more risky elements of the worship service: it can lift up or bring down, shed light or create confusion, evoke thanksgiving or stir up angry rejection. While the speaking skills and theological knowledge of the clergy certainly affect the quality of their overall leadership of a service, it is in the sermon that those gifts—or the lack of them—are revealed most clearly. The sermon is what many people remember most about the service, for good and ill, and the sermon tends to color the understanding of what the Scriptures read that day might mean for those who were listening.

If we are to grow into maturity in our faith, however, it is important to become more than passive listeners to the sermon. While it is perhaps easier to view the sermon as a time during which we should simply be spiritually fed by someone whose job it is to prepare the feast, an adult faith requires more active participation. We are responsible for listening with an open mind and heart, asking questions and making connections to our own lives and our own study of the Bible.

If you are in a parish whose clergy possess strong gifts of preaching, you can be thankful for those gifts and seek to encourage them by your responsive questions and dialogue. If, on the other hand, the sermons usually leave you empty or confused or angry, your job might be to enrich the preaching experience through sharing in Bible studies based on the lectionary texts or in "sermon groups" that gather with the preacher for discussion before or after the sermon. Or perhaps you might reflect on what is missing or going wrong for you: What would *you* have said about these particular readings, if you were the preacher, and why? What "buttons" is the preacher pushing in you, if you find yourself angry or troubled after many sermons? Do you need to talk these over with the preacher or another wise member of the community? If you find the preacher limited in his or her theological or historical knowledge, how can you learn how other Christians have interpreted these readings in the past, and how can you provide your preachers the time needed for study?

No matter how enlightening or deadening you find the sermon fare in your particular parish, the response that is least helpful—to you, to the preacher, and to the congregation as a whole—is to assume the role of detached and passive critic. The sermon can be an enriching interpretive aid to your understanding of the Christian faith found in the Bible, but you must be awake enough to engage and ponder and search for answers to the questions the Bible raises. The sermon is an opportunity for each local congregation to hear *as a body* what the words of Scripture might be saying to them at this moment, in this time. Too many people waste that opportunity by tuning out what they do not want to hear, and by attributing so much authority to the preacher that they deny their own responsibility to think, to respond, to learn.[22]

That said, while the sermon and all the various interpretive aids found in the worship service are important in bringing the readings into the context of our daily lives, hearing the Bible and its interpretation just on Sunday mornings cannot give us an adequate knowledge of the depth and breadth of the biblical witness to God and to God's purposes in the world. A deeper connection with the Bible is needed, through individual study and reflection.

As you become increasing familiar with the writings of the Bible, you will recognize abiding themes that transcend the passage of time: God's faithfulness despite human faithlessness, the covenant between God and humankind, our flawed efforts to connect and reconnect with the God who loves us, our need for redemption and salvation, the actions of God to come among us as savior, the abiding presence of God in our midst. A deeper connection to the literature of the Bible can strengthen our awareness of the ways in which all of this diversity of writing and experience testify to a coherent and consistent message of hope and love, and it will make the lessons heard in worship services more profoundly meaningful. But listening to a few passages on Sunday morning is not enough: we have to open the book, and discover—or rediscover—the richness of the Bible again for ourselves. One of the great rewards of a regular reading of Scripture is the wonderful way in which all of the church's prayers, teachings, and witness become richer and fuller, as these allusions to and uses of the Bible become apparent.

QUESTIONS FOR REFLECTION AND DISCUSSION

1. Turn to "An Order of Worship for the Evening in the Book of Common Prayer," beginning on page 109. Where do you see the influence or images of the Bible? Can you identify what books of the Bible they come from? What are some of the direct quotations of the texts of the Scriptures? Why do you think they were chosen?

2. Choose one or two of your favorite hymns and locate them in the hymnal. What echoes of the texts and images of the Bible do you hear?

3. Think about the ways you have heard the Scriptures interpreted in sermons. What methods were most helpful to you? Why? What confused or frustrated or angered you? Why?

Reading the Bible Again for the First Time

The facets of God's word are more numerous than the faces of those who learn from it. God has hidden within his word all sorts of treasures, so that each of us can be enriched by it from whatever aspect he meditates on. . . . Anyone who encounters scripture should not suppose that the single one of its riches that he has found is the only one to exist; rather, he should realize that he himself is only capable of discovering that one out of the many riches which exist in it.[23]

One of the most difficult habits to unlearn when we approach the Bible again as adults is our relentless effort to search for *the* right answer. As young children we enjoyed our ability to imagine multiple truths in a single world: stories and myths and the things of the spirit were all intertwined with the physical reality of our everyday lives. For most of us, however, as we moved through years of schooling and took hundreds of tests for correct answers, the assumption that there is a single "right" answer to most questions became normative.

So when we come to the Bible as adults, perhaps after we have been away from church and Bible study for some time, we often bring with us the assumption that there is, somewhere, a single, "right" interpretation to the words of Scripture, and therefore the task of Bible study is to find it. Even if we did not have any exposure to the Bible in our childhood, we have certainly been exposed to this idea that the Bible is a book of God's answers to life's questions. It is disconcerting, then, to find that among all the different churches and religious traditions there are widely differing interpretations of the same Bible verses. Furthermore, as we attend the worship services and participate in the life of a particular congregation, we discover that even within the same denomination or congregation, individual Christians can hold radically different understandings of what the Bible says. When Bible study classes deteriorate into arguments about who is right and who is wrong, tensions arise and people feel alienated from one another. Clearly, if the purpose of Bible study is to find a right interpretation of God's word we can all agree on, then the church has failed, since agreement in the church is a very rare thing.

If, on the other hand, the purpose of Bible study is something rather different, then we can let go of the need to settle on a single, correct interpretation, and instead embark on the journey of discovering what the Bible has to say about who God is, and who we are in relationship with God. It will not always be an easy journey: we will be challenged to stretch and perhaps to let go of long-held beliefs and unreflective ways of thinking, as we grow in our knowledge of God and what it means to be fully human, formed in God's image. We will not always find our companions on this journey pleasant or congenial, and we will sometimes fail to be generous with those whom we dislike or with whom we disagree. But the Bible is large enough to encompass us all.

As we have discussed elsewhere in this book, there are myriad ways to read the Bible, each with distinctive strengths and weaknesses. Sometimes we need the support and encouragement of studying the Bible with others; at other times reading alone at our own pace is more helpful. During difficult moments in our lives the familiar and beloved passages of Scripture, especially the Psalms, can be a source of consolation and spiritual comfort. In our more focused times, undertaking the serious study of a book or theme in the Bible can be an intellectual challenge that invigorates and deepens our faith. No single approach will suffice: we need to vary the methods we use in order to see, as Ephrem the Syrian put it, the many different "facets of God's word."

In this chapter we will explore only a few of the methods for reading and studying the Bible that many people of faith have found useful over the centuries. This selection is by no means exhaustive, and we encourage you also to read the many fine books that are available today describing other approaches to the study of Scripture. An annotated list of resources that you might find helpful as you get started is included at the back of this book.

DAILY OFFICES

If you would like to develop a broad understanding of both the Hebrew and Christian Scriptures while deepening your life of prayer, you can hardly find a better pattern to follow than using one of the lectionaries of the church. Christians have long followed the practice of hearing their Scriptures read aloud in worship and at those times in which members of the community have gathered for prayer. In the early church the readings were taken from the Hebrew Scriptures and the letters and teachings of the apostles, some of which eventually became our New Testament.

As the church evolved over the centuries, and especially in the monastic orders who kept the hours of prayer throughout the day, a "schedule" of these readings was developed to encourage communities to read the entire spectrum of books of Scripture, not just their favorite few, and to emphasize the unity of the Christian church as the faithful from many diverse places and communities gathered to read the same lessons on the same day. These daily office lectionaries were the foundation of the services of prayer throughout the day offered by the monastic communities of the Middle Ages, and continue to be a valuable resource for all Christians who pray some form of the daily offices today.

In the 1979 Episcopal Book of Common Prayer we have readings for daily prayer arranged in a Daily Office Lectionary (BCP 933–1,001). While the lectionary is designed to be used primarily in the context of the offices of Morning and Evening Prayer found in the Prayer Book, the readings can also be followed on their own or in the context of other forms of daily prayer, such as the various monastic offices or books of hours that are in print today.[24] The *Daily Office Book* (with readings in the Revised Standard Version of the Bible) and *Contemporary Office Book* (with readings in the New Revised Standard Version) are available from Church Publishing for those who like the ease and simplicity of having the offices and lessons printed in a single volume. You can, of course, use any Bible to follow the readings in the Daily Office Lectionary, though you may find it convenient to keep several bookmarks or ribbons handy, to make it easier to find the various readings day after day.

The notes concerning how to use the Daily Office Lectionary (BCP 934–935) are perhaps more detailed than most of us need for personal reading, but a few notes may be particularly helpful as you get started with using the lectionary. The first paragraph describes how to find out whether you should use the readings for Year One or Year Two: one for odd-numbered years and two for even—though the beginning of the church year in Advent makes this straightforward system a bit more confusing during the month of December!

The notes that follow describe how to incorporate the three lessons provided for each day into two daily offices, or what to do if you pray only one office each day. It is also interesting to note, particularly when the lessons are being read alone at home as part of a regular time of Bible study and not in the context of corporate Morning or Evening Prayer, that "any Reading may be lengthened at discretion." In other words, if you have the time and inclination, you are quite free to read the passages before and after a particular reading—and this is often an important way of deepening your understanding of the passage given for that day. Misinterpreting a passage because we are reading snippets of the Bible out of context is one of the inherent dangers of any lectionary-based system of Bible reading, and remembering to glance at the paragraphs that precede and follow the reading is one way of lessening that risk.

The concluding paragraphs in the Daily Office Lectionary notes concern the readings from the Psalms. In this lectionary portions of the Psalms are read in a seven-week pattern, with some interruptions for feast days in the church year. However, the Prayer Book also offers the alternative for a monthly reading of the Psalms straight through from beginning to end within the pages of the Psalter itself. You will find these thirty-day divisions printed in italics above some psalms: on the first day of the month, for example, you would read Psalms 1 through 5 in the morning and Psalms 6 through 8 in the evening (see BCP 585 and 589). You may find it helpful to try both patterns over the course of several years.

While the lectionary sets forth three readings for each day, along with several psalms, you can also use the lectionary to follow one book at a time. Simply choose one of the three readings listed across the page, and follow that reading down the page, day by day. In this way, you can use this lectionary as a six-year course of studying a large portion of the Bible. As we mentioned in our discussion of the lectionary in the previous chapter, you could also use the readings of Sunday lectionary as a guide for studying the Bible in conjunction with worship, either as a group or as an individual.

READING THROUGH A BOOK OF THE BIBLE

Another approach to reading the Bible is to select a particular book and read it straight through, perhaps a chapter or two each day. This approach has much to recommend it, especially when you are interested in studying a particular book or section of the Bible (such as the Pentateuch or the letters of Paul) in some depth. Reading a book from beginning to end allows you to discover the contexts in which passages you may hear read aloud in worship are found. You also gain a sense of the distinctive "voices" of the authors of the books of the Bible: Paul's letters sound very different from the prophecies of Isaiah; the historical prose of Chronicles tells the story of Israel's relationship with God from a different perspective than the spiritual immediacy of the poetry and prayer of the Psalms; even the gospels tell the same story of the life of Jesus through distinctive voices and points of view.

Annotated study Bibles can be of significant help for this sort of reading. They usually provide an introduction to each book of the Bible that sets the book in its historical context, describe the authors or communities from which it came, and usually summarize the book's main points. Further annotations and comments within the text provide clues to the interpretations of confusing passages or words, identify sections and divisions within the book, and point the way to cross-references of other texts in the Bible that might illuminate the passage in question.

Commentaries are also valuable aids to study, though as when choosing an annotated study Bible, it is worth doing some research about the interpretive slant of the editors and authors of the commentaries you choose to read. Some, like the *New Jerome Biblical Commentary*, are bound in a single volume; most focus on a particular book or books of the Bible—the Anchor Bible series is a good example. Church libraries often have a selection of biblical commentaries to borrow, and having two or even three at hand while you are reading can help balance and inform different interpretations. They range in difficulty from the extremely detailed and learned to the more accessible, so take the time to choose wisely according to what your particular needs are.

It is also helpful to have several translations handy, for as we discussed earlier, each translation of the Bible is in a very real sense an interpretation of the text from a particular perspective. For those who have an interest in biblical Hebrew and Greek, learning enough of those languages to read the books of the Bible in their original language can provide profound insights into the meanings intended by the authors. Even gaining a simple grasp of important vocabulary within a passage can alter the meaning significantly.

Consider the story at the end of John's Gospel, for example, in which the risen Jesus appears to Simon Peter and asks him three times, "Do you love me?" Peter replies yes each time, and we might wonder why Jesus felt the need to ask him three times. Perhaps it is simply a way of letting Peter know that his three denials have been forgiven, as would seem the most obvious interpretation. Yet by using an interlinear Greek-English New Testament, we can see that the Greek word for "love" used in the story changes: the word in Jesus' first two questions is *agapé*, the unconditional love of God. Peter, however, responds with the Greek word for the profound love of human friendship, *phileo*. In Jesus' third question he follows Peter's use of *phileo*, and John notes that "Peter felt hurt" that Jesus had asked him in this way. He replies, "Lord, you know everything;

you know that I love [*phileo*] you." It would be an interesting study to follow this intriguing clue further by understanding more about the different Greek and Hebrew words translated as "love" in English Bibles. A commentary that includes references to the Greek New Testament or Hebrew Scriptures would be useful in this sort of word study.

GROUP STUDY

The convenience of studying the Bible individually at home makes it an attractive way of coming to the Bible as an adult. But most people find it very difficult to develop the discipline necessary to do more serious studies on their own. To gain a deeper connection to God and God's story in the Bible requires regularity and persistence. The Bible is a big book. As the lectionaries indicate, even doing three short readings each day of the year, it takes two years to read most of the Bible—or six years if we read only one passage a day. To nurture a growing relationship with God and God's word will require some consistent work. While some people are able to develop this discipline by themselves, most of us need others to support us, encourage us, and hold us accountable.

It is no accident that the readings assigned in lectionaries were intended to be read in public liturgies. The church long ago discovered that people needed the discipline of joining with others at a specific time and place if they were going to go further in their spiritual journeys with God and God's word. If your church has a daily service of Morning or Evening Prayer, participating in these services regularly can be a good way to develop the practice of making daily connections with the Bible.

A Bible study group can also be a community in which you read the Bible regularly. Many Bible study groups meet weekly or in some other regular pattern, though members of the group might be asked to read the materials to be studied on a daily basis. By being a part of a group of people who are all reading the same material, you gain several advantages. First, you have a weekly reason to do the assigned reading. Even if you are unable to find time daily to read, you should be able to find some time during the week to read the assigned lessons. Second, you have others with whom to discuss the passages. Some of the group may be more familiar with the Bible and can help to explain parts that are difficult, and often a leader will do some research to help the group deepen its understanding. At a minimum, you will have other people of faith who are likewise seeking to know and understand how God is speaking to them in these passages. Third, you have a chance not only to read, but also to *hear* the passages. The practice of silently reading the words of the Bible on a printed page is a relatively recent phenomenon; for centuries the Bible was most often heard aloud in the community of the faithful, who listened together for what God might be saying to them through the Scriptures. It is amazing how just hearing a passage can awaken all kinds of new awareness of meaning and thought.

Reading the Bible with a group helps us develop a discipline of study and can also give us increased confidence in approaching the Bible. The Bible is an intimidating book, and many people find it hard to trust their own interpretations. By reading the Bible with others we come to trust our own ability to understand what the Scriptures are saying, and to learn the church's teachings about the Bible. In this dialogue between the church's teachings and our individual understandings of the Bible, new and deepening insight can take place.

Most Bible study methods, even those intended for individuals, can be adapted for use in groups. Each group needs to develop its own way of entering the Bible, and perhaps to explore several different methods over the course of their meetings.

SOME METHODS OF BIBLE STUDY
Lectio Divina

The practice of prayerfully reading and reflecting on the Bible, both in common worship and in private study, was central to the daily life of the Benedictine monasteries of the Middle Ages. The purpose of this method known as *lectio divina* (holy or godly reading) was not primarily to increase one's knowledge of the Bible in the sense of an intellectual study; rather, monks practiced *lectio divina* as a devotional activity, as a means of being formed and shaped by the word of God.

In the words of the Benedictine scholar Norvene Vest, the foundation for *lectio divina* is "receptive attention." This sort of Scripture reading has the power not only to give new insights into the Bible, but to change our lives. *Lectio* is "the pattern of listening, response, and transformation. *Lectio* draws the reader ever more deeply into the encounter with Christ, which has concrete application in our life in a way that also transcends time."[25] Thus as we read the words of Scripture and reflect on them in the light of the troubles and joys we face on this day, in this moment, we allow God to speak new meanings, new insights. We see implications for our lives that we might never have seen before.

The actual practice of *lectio divina* varies from person to person, but in general it involves the reading of a passage of Scripture and a period of reflection on the words and meaning to be found there for one's life at this particular time. The writings of the Middle Ages often use the image of rumination to describe this process: just as a cow "ruminates" as she repeatedly chews her food, so we "ruminate" over the word of God in Scripture, taking a passage, a phrase, perhaps even one word and turning it over and over in our hearts and minds, all in the context of prayerful openness to God.

One common way of practicing *lectio divina* is to choose a passage from the Bible—which may be from the Daily Office Lectionary, if you are following those readings, or simply the next chapter in whatever book of the Bible you are reading through at this point in time. Begin reading, prayerfully and slowly, and when you come to a word or phrase that attracts your attention, stop. Repeat the word or phrase over and over, perhaps aloud so you can actually *hear* the words. Consider how this word or phrase might touch your life today. Why did it attract your attention? Did you find it troubling? A source of joy or comfort? Puzzling? How do you *feel* as you hear these words over and over again? Then consider what sort of invitation or opening God might be calling you to through this passage. How would you like to respond?[26]

The practice of *lectio divina* can be incorporated into any structure of Bible reading you have undertaken, whether it be lectionary-based or simply reading a book straight through. It is a salutary reminder that our understanding of the Bible needs to be grounded both in a knowledge of the historical-critical methods of study that lead us to the literal meaning of the Scriptures and in an openness to the spiritual and allegorical meanings that form and inform our faith.

Three Senses of Scripture

Episcopal priest and scholar Michael Johnston has described an approach based in the long history of Christian interpretation of the Bible that he has found useful for studying the Bible both in groups and alone.[27] He focuses on what he calls the "three senses of Scripture": the literal, the historical, and the prophetic. No matter what particular method for Bible study is used, part of the study involves discernment of these three senses within the passage under consideration.

The *literal sense* of the passage is what the words of the text actually *say*, quite apart from any interpretation we might lay on them. It can be difficult to separate out the layers of assumptions and interpretations the church has placed on some passages of the Bible over the centuries, especially the more familiar or beloved ones. Johnston asks himself a few clarifying questions when looking for the literal sense: "What does this passage *really* say? Am I conflating the details, or mixing it up with some other passage? Am I bringing some particular point of view or bias to my reading?"[28]

An obvious example of the significance of these layers of interpretation would be the well-known verse from Isaiah that speaks of the "sign" to be given to the house of David: "Look, the young woman is with child and shall bear a son, and shall name him Immanuel" (7:14). In the Greek Septuagint the Hebrew "young woman" is translated as "virgin," and it is this translation that the writer of Matthew's gospel used when he saw in Jesus' birth the fulfillment of this sign: "All this took place to fulfill what had been spoken by the Lord through the prophet: 'Look, the virgin shall conceive and bear a son, and they shall name him Emmanuel,' which means, 'God is with us'" (1:22–23). If we were seeking the literal sense of the passage from Isaiah, however, we would need to consider the Hebrew words themselves, not how they had been translated and interpreted at a later date or how we ourselves might wish to hear them.

The literal sense of the text leads quite naturally to the *historical sense*: What is the historical context in which the passage was written, and what did it mean to the people who heard it then? Knowing the historical context of the passage can inform our understanding of its meaning: some of the Psalms, for example, arose from royal court circles, and it is helpful to know something of the crises that shaped the reigns of the kings of Israel and Judah. Another, often inseparable, aspect of the historical sense is how the passage has been interpreted by people who heard it over the centuries, either as translators or worshipers or scholars. Jesus himself "reinterpreted" the Hebrew Scriptures in his teachings and life, such as when he refuses to stone the woman caught in adultery as would be required by Jewish law, and when he quotes Psalm 22 from the cross.

Likewise, knowing the history of the text itself can deepen our understanding of its historical sense—a study often known as textual criticism. Johnston cites an interesting example in one of Paul's letters, in which he forbids women to speak in church (1 Corinthians 14:33b–6). Since these verses are located in different places in the ancient manuscripts we have of that letter, and since they seem to contradict Paul's thoughts on the equality of women elsewhere in his letters, some scholars believe they were added at a later date, when the church was in the process of narrowing women's opportunities for leadership in the church community.[29] When a word or a passage seems out of place or at odds with other writings, it is important to stop and investigate the history of the text. Sometimes these clues lead to significant changes in how we understand a particular book or writer.

The literal and historical senses both lay the foundation for the *prophetic sense* of Scripture. "To read the Bible for its prophetic sense," writes Michael Johnston, "is to use the text as an instrument for discerning God's presence in our lives now."[30] When we ask questions like "What does this passage mean for us today?" "What is God saying to us in this passage?" "How should I respond to this passage?" we are seeking the prophetic, or spiritual, sense of the text. When the prophetic sense is separated from the literal or historical senses we can find ourselves in realms of interpretation that are not grounded in the revelation of God in the Scriptures but are instead intensely and solely individualistic in meaning. On the other hand, as Johnston summarizes well, the prophetic or spiritual sense is essential for making meaning of the Bible:

> Reading for the literal alone tips toward fundamentalism, risking a future drawn upon an inadequate understanding of the past. But reading for the historical alone leaves us with little more than biblical archaeology; we end up knowing a good deal about ancient Israel but not very much about God. Reading for the spiritual alone tends toward the idiosyncratic and private; it looks to a future cut off from both the past and the present and can lead to strange and intensely personal interpretations. To appropriate the Bible fully, the believing community needs to read it for all three of its senses.[31]

African Bible Study

A popular way of approaching the Bible in churches today is known as the African Bible Study method. There are many variations of this method, which basically provides a way for groups to identify and focus on the three senses of Scriptures described above: the actual words of the passage (the literal sense); its historical context and what it meant for the people to whom the words were written (the historical sense); and its meaning for us today (the prophetic sense). While this approach is designed primarily for studying the Bible in small groups, it can also be adapted for use by individuals or families at home.

Once a passage has been chosen—it might be from a daily lectionary or one of the readings assigned for the next Sunday, or simply one the group would like to study—the members of the group gather in a circle and three people volunteer to read the passage aloud. It is preferable to have a variety of voices, male and female, with a mixture of nationalities and ages, if possible.

After the first reader finishes reading the passage, each person in the group speaks aloud a word, phrase, or sentence that conveys an idea or image from the passage that particularly caught his or her attention. No commentary is allowed at this point, just simple impressions of what the words in the passage actually *say*—in other words, the group is gathering a sense of the literal meaning of the passage.

The second reader then reads the passage again. After this reading, anyone in the group may comment on its content or meaning. This is the time for more in-depth study, and the leader of the group may wish to bring commentaries, linguistic aids, and alternative translations into the discussion at this point. How did the original hearers of the passage interpret its meaning? Are there confusing or intriguing words we need to investigate? What can the historical context tell us? The group may wish to have on hand Bibles or written copies of the passage at this stage to enhance their study, since we are not as adept as our forebears in memorizing oral stories.

Finally, once the group has explored the historical and literal senses of the passage, the third reader again reads the passage aloud. Each member of the group then speaks aloud some sort of prayer or insight or desire for transformation gained through the hearing and studying of this passage. These prayers and reflections are then gathered by the group leader into a closing collect, reminding us that reading the Bible in the Christian community is always inextricably intertwined with prayer and transformation within the body of Christ.

Thematic Studies of Scripture

Another way to approach the Bible is to ask what it has to say about a particular topic, such as "righteousness" or "grace." This is a somewhat more challenging way to look at Scripture, and it can provide valuable insights for our understanding of the biblical story.

To undertake this kind of study, a couple of reference materials are helpful. First, locate a concordance. A concordance lists words from the Bible alphabetically and gives all or the most important places those words appear in the Bible. The bigger the concordance, the more complete the list of words. Along with the words themselves a concordance usually also provides a small portion of the verses in which the words appear. It may also indicate if there is more than one Hebrew or Greek root to the English translation.

If your theme is based upon a word, say "peace," you could look up the references to this word in a concordance and then compare the various ways it is used. In this case you might find that both Hebrew and Greek have a major word that is translated as "peace" in English Bibles, but that there are also a couple of other terms that may also be translated "peace" in the sense of keeping silent (or "holding one's peace"). You would find only a few references to these minor words, but a long series of passages from many books of the Bible using the major words for "peace." By examining these texts a group or an individual could come to a much deeper understanding of what the Bible means when it speaks of the "peace of God."

Another helpful reference is a "wordbook" or Bible dictionary. Like a concordance, a Bible dictionary is arranged in alphabetical order, but rather than just listing all the passages in which the word appears, it will also offer a commentary on the meaning and biblical usage of the word or theme.

Such a thematic study of Scripture can be fruitful if the theme is one about which the Bible has something to say—of which there are many. But there are also themes that you would not find in the Bible in the direct sense of specific words used to speak about that theme. If you wanted to know what the Bible has to say about "creation," for example, you would find only a few references to that specific word in a concordance, while in a Bible dictionary you would find other more general references to the theme of creation in the Scriptures.

One word of caution. While these and other reference books can be helpful, they need to be used carefully. Often they will have their own particular descriptions of a theme or word. These insights can be helpful, but if you substitute reading *about* a theme for taking the time to locate the biblical references and reading them yourself, you risk coming only to the conclusions of a particular author and not to your own understanding. And, of course, the point of such a study is to come to know the Bible, not someone else's description of the Bible. The perceptions of other people, especially those who have a deep and scholarly knowledge of the Bible, will be helpful in filling in your own understanding, but the Bible must be the main text for study.

Literature Studies

Another way to come to a study of Scripture is to look at various kinds of biblical literature. As we have mentioned earlier, there are many kinds of literature in the Bible, and the ways in which biblical ideas and themes are presented is an important factor in understanding them. For example, a study of one of Paul's letters could well include some reflection on letter writing as a form of communication. The fact that Paul wrote in letters tells us something about his purpose and method. While his letters contain a great deal of what we think of as "doctrine," clearly Paul was not writing treatises or theological tomes. He chose to write letters, not gospels. His purpose was to address the situations in his churches, so his theological teachings come in the context of his reflection on what is actually happening, what is being said and taught in the congregations to whom he writes. Looking at Paul's teachings from this perspective can clarify some of his ideas and help create a context for his teachings that can be helpful in applying them to contemporary affairs.

Examining the kinds of literature in a biblical book or a section of a biblical book can be as important as looking at the words as you seek a perspective on the Bible's message. It can also help to illuminate the ways in which the people who wrote the Bible (and those to whom they wrote) thought about God and faith in their time. We can become more aware of how God communicates to his people through a variety of media. You may find that certain kinds of literature in the Bible speak more clearly to you than others. Perhaps poetry appeals to your way of thinking, or maybe you like stories or parables better. It may be that you prefer dialogue and discussion, or you may be the sort of person who likes difficult or abstract ideas. These are all present in the Scriptures, and finding them can help to draw you into the biblical story, thus leading you into a deeper connection with the Bible.

The Bible in the Arts

An interesting way to deepen an awareness of the Bible is to look at how the Bible has been used in literature and other art forms. Many poets and novelists throughout the history of western art have taken biblical themes as topics for their works. Among contemporary writers, John Steinbeck, William Faulkner, Frederick Buechner, Flannery O'Connor, John Updike, Annie Dillard, and others have written novels or short stories based upon biblical stories or ideas. Poets such as T. S. Eliot, W. H. Auden, and William Butler Yeats have likewise written poetry incorporating biblical themes and tales, and many artists, sculptors, and iconographers have portrayed biblical scenes or characters. These art forms can be ways for a group to begin to find connections with the biblical materials. In a sense, it is coming to Bible study from a different direction: instead of asking what the Bible says about our contemporary experience, we ask our experience and culture to lead us to and help us understand in a new way certain biblical truths or ideas.

For example, there are several interesting studies of Rembrandt's famous painting of *The Prodigal Son*. By spending time looking at this painting—examining the people, discerning their attitudes, the expressions on their faces, and their connections with one another—the parable that Jesus tells in Luke 15:11–32 is brought to life in a new way. We can move from the simple words of the story to a deeper, more emotional engagement with the characters of the story. We see more clearly the God who is revealed in the parable, and we see ourselves more clearly, too.

Similarly, some of Flannery O'Connor's short stories can make interesting connections between the real world we live in and the world of the Bible. The poems of T. S. Eliot or the music of Bach or Mozart can also offer possibilities for experiencing various ways the biblical story has been expressed over time—expressions that go beyond the simple words of Scripture and speak not just to our minds, but to our hearts and our spirits as well.

In the past few years a number of films have been produced that are directly connected to the biblical story, often arousing considerable controversy among people of faith. *The Passion of the Christ* is perhaps the most recent, but there are also films based on Jesus' parables, the book of Revelation, and the Exodus story. While there have been many attempts to create a visual telling of the stories of the Bible over the decades, with varying degrees of success, many films use such broader biblical themes as love, grace, redemption, and hope as a basis for telling a contemporary tale, one that evokes the Bible's voice without trying to reproduce it—perhaps sometimes even without realizing the universal themes conveyed are found in the Scriptures. These films often make for the best discussions and can be interesting ways to discover how Scripture actually speaks in the contemporary world.

JUST DO IT

So how do we approach, perhaps for the first time, a book that has engendered so many different methods of study and has fostered the development of an enormous library of supplementary resources and reference books? We just do it. We open the pages and start reading. Even if the words seem obscure or the stories strange, we keep reading. We ask questions. Talk with other people. Listen to sermons. Find resources to help us. But above all, we keep reading. We are never reading alone in our reading of the Bible, for as Jesus told his disciples, God's Holy Spirit dwells within us to guide us into all truth (John 16:13). And so we trust that no matter how sketchy or inadequate our knowledge of the Bible is now, we will still be able to hear God's word in these sometimes obscure or strange words. What matters is simply that we open this big, intimidating, wonderful book—and listen with our ears attuned and our eyes open to see the God revealed there.

Questions for Reflection and Discussion

1. Choose one or more of the following passages, or one of your own choosing, to try with these methods of study:

Lectio divina: 1 Corinthians 13 (Paul's hymn to love)

Three senses of Scripture: Luke 1:46–55 (the Magnificat)

African method: Matthew 5:1–12 (the Beatitudes). You might try using three different translations for this well-known passage.

Thematic word study: Use a concordance to look up passages containing the word "righteousness" and compare them. What biblical definitions of this concept do you find? Other words you might try include "wealth," "justice," and "holy."

2. What works of art or literature do you know that have biblical themes or images? If you can identify the passages or sections of Scripture to which they refer, look those passages up in a Bible. What can you learn from the context in which they are found?

3. Read John 14:6, in which Jesus tells his disciples that "no one comes to the Father except through me." What are some possible ways of understanding the meaning of this statement in the context of a world in which there are many different religions? What Bible study methods might be helpful in developing an interpretation of this passage?

Notes

1. Quoted in Rowan Williams, *Where God Happens: Discovering Christ in One Another* (Boston: New Seeds, 2005), 158.

2. For a more detailed introduction to the Episcopal Prayer Book, see *Welcome to the Book of Common Prayer* by Vicki K. Black (Harrisburg, PA: Morehouse Publishing, 2005).

3. Marion J. Hatchett, *Commentary on the American Prayer Book* (New York: Seabury Press, 1980), 195.

4. Quoted in Jaroslav Pelikan, *Whose Bible Is It? A History of the Scriptures Through the Ages* (New York: Viking, 2005), 18.

5. Verna J. Dozier, *The Dream of God* (New York: Church Publishing, 1991, 2006), 9.

6. Frederick Buechner, *Wishful Thinking: A Theological ABC* (New York: Harper & Row, 1973), 65.

7. For an excellent discussion of the role translators play in interpreting the meaning of Bible texts, see Donald Kraus, *Choosing a Bible: For Worship, Teaching, Study, Preaching, and Prayer* (New York: Church Publishing, 2006).

8. Benjamin D. Sommer, "Inner-biblical Interpretation," in *The Jewish Study Bible*, Adele Berlin and Marc Zvi Brettler, eds. (New York: Oxford University Press, 2004), 1,829.

9. Augustine, *On Christian Doctrine*, I.36.40, quoted in *Scripture: An Ecumenical Introduction to the Bible and its*

Interpretation, ed. Michael J. Gorman (Peabody, MA: Hendrickson Publishers, 2005), 138.

10. Thomas Aquinas, *Summa of Theology*, quoted in Pelikan, *Whose Bible Is It?*, 127.

11. Quoted in Pelikan, *Whose Bible Is It?*, 131.

12. Ibid., 167.

13. L. William Countryman, *Biblical Authority or Biblical Tyranny? Scripture and the Christian Pilgrimage* (Cambridge, MA: Cowley Publications, 1994), 41.

14. Ibid., 53–57, 79.

15. See the excellent discussion in Alan Jones, *Common Prayer on Common Ground: A Vision of Anglican Orthodoxy* (Harrisburg, PA: Morehouse Publishing, 2006).

16. Thomas C. Brownell (Bishop of Connecticut), *The Family Prayer Book* (New York: n.p., 1857), 14.

17. Hatchett, *Commentary on the American Prayer Book*, 203.

18. Other psalms that are paraphrased are listed on page 940 in *The Hymnal 1982*. In the supplemental hymnals of the Episcopal Church, *Wonder, Love and Praise* and *Lift Every Voice and Sing II*, similar indexes of scriptural references can be found.

19. Hymn 685 in *The Hymnal 1982* (New York: Church Publishing, 1985). Words by Augustus Montague Toplady (1740–1778).

20. For more information about the lectionary and the seasons of the church year, see other books in this series: Vicki Black, *Welcome to the Church Year* (Harrisburg, PA: Morehouse Publishing, 2004) and Vicki Black, *Welcome to the Book of Common Prayer* (Harrisburg, PA: Morehouse Publishing, 2005).

21. Pelikan, *Whose Bible Is It?*, 125.

22. An excellent book on the listening dimension to the sermon is David Schlafer, *Surviving the Sermon: A Guide to Preaching for Those Who Have to Listen* (Cambridge, MA: Cowley Publications, 1992).

23. Ephrem the Syrian, *Commentary on the Diatessaron*, in *The Luminous Eye: The Spiritual World Vision of St. Ephrem*, trans. Sebastian Brock (Kalamazoo, MI: Cistercian Publications, 1992), 50–51.

24. See, for example, Phyllis Tickle's several volumes of *The Divine Hours*, published by Doubleday, and *The Saint Helena Breviary: Personal Edition* (New York: Church Publishing, 2006).

25. Norvene Vest, *No Moment Too Small: Rhythms of Silence, Prayer, and Holy Reading* (Boston, MA: Cowley Publications, 1994), 71, 78.

26. For further examples of *lectio divina*, see chapter 2 in Vest's *No Moment Too Small*.

27. Michael Johnston, *Engaging the Word*, vol. 3, New Church's Teaching Series (Cambridge, MA: Cowley Publications, 1998).

28. Ibid., 45.

29. Ibid., 47–48.

30. Ibid., 51.

31. Ibid., 53.

Resources

INTRODUCTIONS TO THE BIBLE

Brown, Raymond E. *An Introduction to the New Testament*. New York: Doubleday, 1997.

Brueggemann, Walter. *An Introduction to the Old Testament: The Canon and Christian Imagination*. Louisville, KY: Westminster John Knox, 2003.

Buehrens, John A. *Understanding the Bible: An Introduction for Skeptics, Seekers and Religious Liberals*. Boston: Beacon Press, 2003.

Carmody, Timothy R. *Reading the Bible: A Study Guide*. New York: Paulist Press, 2004.

Davis, Ellen F. *Getting Involved With God: Rediscovering the Old Testament*. Cambridge, MA: Cowley Publications, 2001.

Ehrman, Bart D. *A Brief Introduction to the New Testament*. New York: Oxford University Press, 2004.

————. *The New Testament: A Historical Introduction to the Early Christian Writings*. New York: Oxford University Press, 2004.

Faley, Roland J., TOR. *From Genesis to Apocalypse*. New York: Paulist Press, 2005.

Fant, Clyde E., Donald W. Musser, and Mitchell G. Reddish. *An Introduction to the Bible*. Rev. ed. Nashville, TN: Abingdon Press, 2001.

Harrington, Daniel J., SJ. *Invitation to the Apocrypha*. Grand Rapids, MI: Eerdmans, 1999.

Jones, Ivor H. *The Apocrypha*. Peterborough, England: Epworth Press, 2003.

Riches, John. *The Bible: A Very Short Introduction*. New York: Oxford University Press, 2000.

Witherington, Ben. *The New Testament Story*. Grand Rapids, MI: Eerdmans, 2004.

GENERAL READING

Anderson, Bernhard W. *Understanding the Old Testament*. 4th ed. Englewood Cliffs, NJ: Prentice-Hall, 1986.

Brueggemann, Walter. *The Book That Breathes New Life: Scriptural Authority and Biblical Theology*. Minneapolis, MN: Fortress, 2004.

Countryman, L. William. *Biblical Authority or Biblical Tyranny? Scripture and the Christian Pilgrimage*. Cambridge, MA: Cowley Publications, 1994.

Court, John M. *Biblical Interpretation: The Meaning of Scripture, Past and Present*. London: T & T Clark, 2004.

Ferlo, Roger. *Opening the Bible*. Vol. 2. New Church's Teaching Series. Cambridge, MA: Cowley Publications, 1997.

Gorman, Michael J., ed. *Scripture: An Ecumenical Introduction to the Bible and its Interpretation*. Peabody, MA: Hendrickson Publishers, 2005.

Johnston, Michael. *Engaging the Word*. Vol. 3. New Church's Teaching Series. Cambridge, MA: Cowley Publications, 1998.

Kraus, Donald. *Choosing a Bible: For Worship, Teaching, Study, Preaching, and Prayer*. New York: Church Publishing, 2006.

Pelikan, Jaroslav. *Whose Bible Is It? A History of the Scriptures Through the Ages*. New York: Viking, 2005.

A SELECTION OF ENGLISH VERSIONS
OF THE BIBLE TODAY

The New Revised Standard Version (1989)

This is the version of the Bible most often read in Episcopal churches. It is a revision of the Revised Standard Version, which continued the traditions of the King James Version. The translators had two objects in mind. First, to bring the latest information from scholars to their work so that their translation is accurate and faithful to the original texts; and, second, to use more inclusive language to make the reading more accessible to everyone. Thus, when the word "men" is used in the text to refer to men and women, this translation uses a more inclusive term, like "people" or "humankind." When people are addressed as "brothers," this translation usually renders the phrase as "brothers and sisters." Because it was written with the traditions of the King James Version in mind, it reads aloud well, and that, as well as the inclusive language, accounts for its use in many churches.

You can also find this translation in study versions of the Bible. *The New Oxford Annotated Bible* and the *Harper Collins Study Bible*, among others, use this translation and then include introductory materials, as well as notes on the text and information about translators' choices of words. These Bibles also often have references that indicate when other portions of the Bible are being quoted or referred to.

The New American Standard Bible (1971)

The American Standard Bible is a translation done in the early part of the twentieth century, and was a precursor of the Revised Standard Version. The New American Standard Bible was published by the Lochman Foundation in 1971, and is a very literal translation of the Hebrew and Greek texts. Because it is a word-for-word translation, it is especially useful for students of the Bible, but it does not read well aloud, since its renderings are often stilted and obscure. This Bible is also published in an updated edition, with revisions of some of the outdated language and some indications of textual difficulties.

The Revised English Bible (1989)

The New English Bible was published in 1970, and was a product of the universities and scholars in Great Britain. Written to bring a modern British translation to the churches of the British Isles, it was a fresh translation of the Greek and Hebrew texts into contemporary British English, which makes it somewhat difficult for American readers, since it contains British colloquialisms.

In the 1980s a revision was planned to eliminate some of these, and to use more inclusive language. Because of its attempts to render the translation in contemporary idiom, the new work is not as literal a translation as other versions and contains attempts to paraphrase more clearly the meaning of the text. One of the unique characteristics of this Bible (in contrast to other recent translations) is the absence of "titles" for sections of each book. Instead, the text is presented without breaks. This version is also heard in Episcopal churches, and certainly in the churches of the Church of England. A translation of the Apocrypha is also included in this Bible.

The New Jerusalem Bible (1985)

The Jerusalem Bible was first published in 1970, a year in which several new translations of the Bible emerged. It was a result of the work of French Dominicans, who brought into being a new French translation of the Roman Catholic Bible that was not based on Jerome's Latin Vulgate, but rather on the original Greek and Hebrew texts. The English version was done by British Roman Catholic scholars, though based on the French scholarship, using the original languages as well as the French text. It is the first complete Roman Catholic Bible in English to be translated from the original languages.

The scholarly introductions and notes in this Bible are outstanding and offer Bible students a rich source of information and understanding. A revision of the Jerusalem Bible was undertaken in the mid-1980s and was an attempt to move beyond the French translation and also to correct some of the interpretive renderings in the text. A Reader's Edition was published in 1989, providing a version of the text without the scholarly commentary and notes.

The New International Version (1978)

Published by the International Bible Society, this version is a very readable text, and has a high quality of literary prose. It was produced by a group of conservative biblical scholars from the evangelical churches who were not altogether happy with the

Revised Standard Version and who wanted a version that was more in keeping with their theological views. The translators were concerned to render the text as a faithful translation of "God's Word in written form." This version tends to be more colloquial in its English, more faithful to the original texts, and a good literary rendering of the text into English.

The Good News Bible (Today's English Version) (1976)

This Bible was produced by the American Bible Society and was intended for use by missionaries in countries where English was a second language, and so was written primarily for persons with a third- or fourth-grade level of English comprehension. As a result, it is not a word-for-word (or literal) translation of the original texts, but is an attempt to render the meaning of those texts in contemporary American English. It also attempts to alter some of the archaic customs and idioms of the Bible and to communicate their meaning in more modern idioms and expressions. A similar version—not a revision, but a new translation—called the Contemporary English Version, also using simple English vocabulary, was published in 1995.

The Living Bible (1971)

This version of the Bible is a paraphrase of the American Standard Version of the Bible (1901) by Kenneth N. Taylor. A *paraphrase version* means that the author did not work from the original languages, but rather worked from a current translation and tried to render the English in such a way as to make the text clearer. In this case, Taylor began by rendering a text for his children during family devotions, but went on to clarify the text from a "rigid evangelical position." He frequently uses evangelical terms and clichés from the revivalist tradition, since his purpose was to bring evangelical doctrines and scriptural meanings to the fore. The text is often expanded in order to clarify what was written in the original text. While this does sometimes help clarify a biblical story, idea, or concept, it may be difficult for a reader to discern what is original and what is the author's work. It also leaves the reader without the freedom to interpret or seek a clearer meaning independently. This is a very popular version because the simple, straightforward American English is easy to understand. It can be a helpful study resource, but generally should be read along with an accurate translation, so the interpretations and expansions can be seen and identified.

This version was reissued in 1996 as the *New Living Translation*, a revisiting of Taylor's work by a group of evangelical scholars, who worked from the original languages to render a version in the vocabulary and language of the "average" person.

The Message (2000)

The Message is another attempt to paraphrase the Bible in contemporary terms and language, this time by Eugene H. Peterson. While he worked with the original languages, according to Peterson his work was not to "render a word-for-word conversion of Greek into English, but rather to convert the tone, the rhythm, and the events, the ideas, into ways we actually think and speak." As with *The Living Bible*, this vivid and lively paraphrase may help clarify the meaning and intent of the Bible, and is useful as a companion to a good translation, if the reader is aware that the interpretations are those of Peterson and not the authors of the texts.

REFERENCE BOOKS AND STUDY BIBLES

The Anchor Bible Series

These substantial volumes, published by Doubleday, offer a book-by-book translation of all the books in the Old and New Testaments and the Apocrypha, each written by a biblical scholar. They can be found in most good church or theological libraries, and are a valuable resource for the study of a particular book or passage in the Bible.

Anglican Association of Biblical Scholars Study Series

These volumes of "Conversations with Scripture," published by Morehouse, are written by scholars in a style that is accessible for parish studies. Each volume discusses a theme, such as the parables of Jesus, or a particular book of the Bible, such as the book of Revelation.

Berlin, Adele, and Marc Zvi Brettler, eds. *The Jewish Study Bible: Jewish Publication Society Tanakh Translation*. New York: Oxford University Press, 2004.

Brown, Raymond E., S.S., Joseph A. Fitzmyer, S.J., and Roland E. Murphy, O.Carm., eds. *The New Jerome Biblical Commentary*. Englewood Cliffs, NJ: Prentice-Hall, 1990.

Browning, W. R. F. *A Dictionary of the Bible*. Oxford: Oxford University Press, 2004.

Metzger, Bruce M., and Roland E. Murphy, eds. *The New Oxford Annotated Bible with the Apocrypha: New Revised Standard Version*. New York: Oxford University Press, 1991.